5-Star Review by Read

Organizational Development Essentials You Always Wanted to Know by Ankur Mithal combines knowledge and experience in an excellent overview of Organizational Development (OD). For those who are interested in utilizing Organizational Development in their professional work, studying the subject, or interested in how to bring change into an organization, this is an excellent overview and introduction to the subject. The author's experience in building multicultural teams and working as an international consultant definitely shows in the explanation of the subject matter. He introduces important techniques such as Fishbone Analysis, Content Analysis, and Force Field Analysis along with a variety of perspectives in developing the action plan. He also introduces basic statistics and uses to help diagnose the problem using an OD approach. The book concludes with an invitation to those interested in becoming an OD professional with an excellent overview of the skills, knowledge, and abilities for success as a consultant or part of an organization.

Ankur Mithal introduces the world of OD in Organizational Development Essentials You Always Wanted to Know in a very effective and interesting manner. The book is practical and well-organized in its approach, explaining the basics of Organizational Development and change management in a very interesting manner. The challenges of institutionalizing change management are important and well explained, urging the reader to learn more about this subject. There are quizzes at the end of each chapter that review the basic concepts along with a chapter summary. For those interested in pursuing a career in Organizational Development, Mr. Mithal provides an excellent explanation of OD's importance in bringing about change and the knowledge, skills, and abilities to be successful. A very useful book and highly recommended to those interested in learning more about bringing about change in their organizations.

SELF-LEARNING MANAGEMENT SERIES

VIBRANT
PUBLISHERS

ORGANIZATIONAL DEVELOPMENT ESSENTIALS

YOU ALWAYS WANTED TO KNOW

An insight into the evolving discipline of Organizational Development and the process of implementing an intervention under it.

ANKUR MITHAL

Organizational Development
Essentials You Always Wanted To Know
First Edition

Paperback ISBN 10: 1-63651-148-1
Paperback ISBN 13: 978-1-63651-148-1

Ebook ISBN 10: 1-63651-149-X
Ebook ISBN 13: 978-1-63651-149-8

Hardback ISBN 10: 1-63651-150-3
Hardback ISBN 13: 978-1-63651-150-4

Library of Congress Control Number: 2022947351

Vibrant Publishers books are available at special quantity discount for sales promotions, or for use in corporate training programs. For more information please write to bulkorders@vibrantpublishers.com

Please email feedback / corrections (technical, grammatical or spelling) to spellerrors@vibrantpublishers.com

To access the complete catalogue of Vibrant Publishers, visit www.vibrantpublishers.com

SELF-LEARNING MANAGEMENT SERIES

TITLE	PAPERBACK* ISBN

ACCOUNTING, FINANCE & ECONOMICS

COST ACCOUNTING AND MANAGEMENT ESSENTIALS	9781636511030
FINANCIAL ACCOUNTING ESSENTIALS	9781636510972
FINANCIAL MANAGEMENT ESSENTIALS	9781636511009
MACROECONOMICS ESSENTIALS	9781636511818
MICROECONOMICS ESSENTIALS	9781636511153
PERSONAL FINANCE ESSENTIALS	9781636511849

ENTREPRENEURSHIP & STRATEGY

BUSINESS PLAN ESSENTIALS	9781636511214
BUSINESS STRATEGY ESSENTIALS	9781949395778
ENTREPRENEURSHIP ESSENTIALS	9781636511603

GENERAL MANAGEMENT

BUSINESS LAW ESSENTIALS	9781636511702
DECISION MAKING ESSENTIALS	9781636510026
LEADERSHIP ESSENTIALS	9781636510316
PRINCIPLES OF MANAGEMENT ESSENTIALS	9781636511542
TIME MANAGEMENT ESSENTIALS	9781636511665

*Also available in Hardback & Ebook formats

SELF-LEARNING MANAGEMENT SERIES

TITLE	PAPERBACK* ISBN
HUMAN RESOURCE MANAGEMENT	
DIVERSITY IN THE WORKPLACE ESSENTIALS	9781636511122
HR ANALYTICS ESSENTIALS	9781636510347
HUMAN RESOURCE MANAGEMENT ESSENTIALS	9781949395839
ORGANIZATIONAL BEHAVIOR ESSENTIALS	9781636510378
ORGANIZATIONAL DEVELOPMENT ESSENTIALS	9781636511481
MARKETING & SALES MANAGEMENT	
DIGITAL MARKETING ESSENTIALS	9781949395747
MARKETING MANAGEMENT ESSENTIALS	9781636511788
SALES MANAGEMENT ESSENTIALS	9781636510743
SERVICES MARKETING ESSENTIALS	9781636511733
OPERATIONS & PROJECT MANAGEMENT	
AGILE ESSENTIALS	9781636510057
OPERATIONS & SUPPLY CHAIN MANAGEMENT ESSENTIALS	9781949395242
PROJECT MANAGEMENT ESSENTIALS	9781636510712
STAKEHOLDER ENGAGEMENT ESSENTIALS	9781636511511

*Also available in Hardback & Ebook formats

About the Author

Ankur Mithal is a widely experienced business professional. In over 15 years with Standard Chartered Bank, he worked in Sales, Project Management as well as Operations, operating out of Kolkata, Delhi, Hong Kong, Mumbai, and Singapore at different points and leading cross-border multicultural teams. Thereafter, in the BPO industry, he led delivery for leading clients of IBM Daksh and HCL BPO. He was involved in a number of improvement interventions in the BPO industry that straddled the disciplines of Organizational Development as well as Quality which created interest and enabled him to learn about them.

Thereafter, he became an entrepreneur and launched workreadyknowledge.com, an E-learning venture, and vdohire.com, a Digital hiring venture. He has also worked as the COO of Action for Autism, a Delhi-based non-profit.

He has authored books like Some Method Some Madness, Managing BPO in India - a guide to the BPO industry and What Happens in Office, Stays in Office – a collection of satirical stories about office life.

Ankur operates as a business consultant and a freelance writer apart from working on his own writing projects.

Other contributors

We would like to thank our editor, Denean Robinson for her contribution to making this book the best version possible. Denean holds a BS. Degree in Family Studies and Counseling, a master's degree in Executive Management from the University of Maryland University College, and a doctoral degree in Educational Leadership from Argosy University in Arlington, Virginia.

Dr. Robinson over the last seventeen years has been developing and facilitating Marketing, Human Resource Development, Organizational Behavior, Organizational Development, and Change Management courses/seminars at various universities and organizations across the Washington, DC metropolitan area. In addition, Dr. Robinson has developed customized curriculums and educational programs for various state government and private agencies in the areas of career development, personal management, and strategic planning. In 2010, Dr. Robinson began to receive personal invitations from Chapter Presidents to present Human Resources/Executive Training courses to various Society of Human Resource Management Chapters across the country.

What experts say about this book!

This book uses a general model of planned change like the Quality management framework: Entry, Diagnosis, Implementation, Evaluation, and Institutionalization. The model allows the reader to understand each phase of the OD process. The language of the book is easy to understand and it includes summaries and quizzes at the end of each chapter. It also includes a useful OD proposal in section 4.4. This book is useful for undergraduate and graduate students and can be used in Organizational Development and Organizational Behavior courses.

– Rodolfo Biasca, Professor of Economics,
Purdue University Global

The book is well structured and written in a style that is easy to read and comprehend. In the first three chapters, the book traces the beginning and evolution of OD, it's relevance, challenges, and excitement experienced by an OD practitioner, how it differs from Change Management and other seemingly related fields. The next five chapters provide an overview of a typical OD intervention. The final chapter is from the practitioner's perspective, covering the essential knowledge, skills, and ethics that an OD practitioner must possess and practice.

The book will benefit young aspirants wanting to build a career in OD. It provides useful perspectives to trainers and early stage consultants who wish to explore OD as a field of practice. It will also serve as an informative source for non OD professionals supporting OD interventions. The essential message of the book is that organizations should not react to change but embrace, engage and manage it.

– Umesh Dhand, Faculty,
SPJIMR

What experts say about this book!

The book was easily understandable and is applicable to all levels of crowd. The quiz given at the end of each topic is much appreciated. It is indeed a good idea for better understanding and review for the learners. The book can be recommended to students, entrepreneurs and also to people who do distance-learning.

– Dr. K. R. Kolammal, Assistant Professor,
MOP Vaishnav College of women

Organizational Development Essentials is well written with ample illustrations. The scientific and structured approach and the simple and expressive language make this book a good read for beginners as well as experts.

– Prof. Abhijit Khurape, Management Faculty,
AISSMS Institute of Management

As an MBA professor that teaches courses on Organizational Change Management, I found this book to be particularly interesting and resourceful. Not only was the content concise and clear, but it was also perfectly detailed and thorough enough to complement any undergraduate or graduate course in organizational change management strategy or just general business management. It's also the perfect resource for a professional newly appointed to management positions— regardless of the job level or corporate size. It provides specific action items on how to approach change, the very steps that I teach in my courses. Very impressed with this book and I will be recommending it to my graduate students.

– Shelly Nice, Adjunct Professor,
Southern New Hampshire University

What experts say about this book!

Organizational Development Essentials You Always Wanted To Know covers all the essential aspects that a learner must know about organizational development. The conceptualization is apt and relevant to the requirements of the current generation. The content provides a broader perspective of organizational development to the student community and intriguing insights to learners from the industry.

– P.Reshma, Assistant Professor (HR & OB), Dept of Management Studies, The American College

The book gives a very comprehensive and effective understanding of the concepts and interventions of Organizational Development (OD). The author's lucid writing style will keep the readers interested. It can truly be called a book for practitioners as well as HR Professionals entering in this area. In the VUCA world of today, where "Change is the only constant" and the organizations need to adapt to the change, this book in its simplistic style is the need of the hour.

– Dr. Neera Singh, Associate Professor, Shanti Business School

This book is a comprehensive guide for all HR professionals and those aspiring to join the HR profession. The nine chapters of the book include organizational examples that illuminate the readers with corporate insights and have interesting quizzes at the end of each chapter. The book is also recommended for OD consultants who aim to guide the honchos.

– Ms. Jyoti Kukreja, Assistant Professor, Jagannath International Management School

What experts say about this book!

The book is both educational and interesting and the content is reader-friendly. The author manages to turn a rarely understood management task into a clear and exciting field. Current examples (i.e. the Ship Evergreen getting stuck in the Suez Canal and blocking traffic) further illustrate each chapter. Modern principles of management, such as the rewards of treating people with respect and creating autonomy and purpose are used throughout, making the text a useful tool for the new generation of employees.

"What OD is not" is didactic and puts the focus on what it really is. The Sample OD Proposal is a brilliant and clear example of applied tools for readers/students. The quizzes with answers help to reinforce the learnings.

– Fernando Pargas, Dept of Management,
James Madison University

Organizational Development Essentials You Always Wanted To Know is a comprehensive book written in a crisp language and covers the essentials of the subject. This book is ideally suited as a reference text book for management students at the undergraduate level. The short cases as part of each chapter to elaborate on concepts makes learning easy and effective. The quiz provided at the end of each chapter is a good tool to check the understanding level of the readers. Overall, the book is good for beginners who wish to understand the basic concepts of Organizational Development.

– Vidhya Thakkar, Associate Professor,
Somaiya Vidyavihar University

Table of Contents

This page is intentionally left blank

Preface

As an evolving discipline, Organizational Development is finding interest among people who work for organizations as well as youngsters who are exploring career options for themselves. OD professionals could even have an opportunity of shaping the future of the discipline.

The remit is vast. As development could come in any shape or form, the discipline does not lend itself easily to be defined by boundaries, though many experts who have been involved with developments in the early stages have made attempts to give it a definite shape and form. However, that is still a work in progress.

That is part of the challenge as well as the excitement of OD. While on the one hand, practitioners might struggle to define what they do for a living, on the other hand, the prospect of each intervention being unique, and the possibility of operating in a dynamic and ever-changing environment, is attractive.

The book serves to provide an overview of the discipline and the contributions made by past experts. It also provides an overview of the key steps at each stage as one goes about implementing an OD intervention.

This page is intentionally left blank

Introduction

In sports, old records keep falling and new ones get created. In life and in business, human beings continue to strive for more, contributing to the change happening around us.

"Change is the only constant" is a phrase we hear often and is believed to be coined by the Greek philosopher Heraclitus. And we are witness to the impact all around us. The world is in constant flux as change has become constant. It is true as much to individuals as it is to organizations.

Some people and organizations create change. Some have change thrust upon them as a result of developments around them. In either situation, change happens and they need to manage it and learn to cope with it, or perish.

Survival being a key instinct of both humans and organizations, the process of handling the challenges posed by change has been underway for many decades and has come to be known as the discipline of Organizational Development, or OD.

Organizational Development introduces the concept of planned change as a desirable goal, as opposed to change that is thrust upon the organization. There are several theories on handling planned change proposed by many experts in the field.

The sequence of activities that result in achieving a desired goal or state has come to be referred to as an intervention. The process of managing them is referred to as the implementation of an intervention.

What has also emerged over the years is a common process or sequence that can be followed by OD experts and leaders while proposing and implementing an OD intervention. This common process has been laid out in detail in the book.

By the end of this book, you should be in a position to understand the following:

- What is Organizational Development and its key characteristics
- Core values and goals of OD
- Factors that are causing change
- Moving from reactive to planned change
- Evolution and growth of OD with a discussion on pioneers and their proposed models
- Handling an intervention through its key stages of:
  1. Entry
  2. Diagnosis
  3. Implementation
  4. Evaluation
  5. Institutionalization
- The making of an OD professional

Who can benefit from the book?

The book can be useful for a cross-section of people.

- For a management professional, it would open up streams of thought in terms of how change could be introduced in the organization in a managed way.

- For an OD professional, it should serve as a refresher of some of the core concepts of the discipline as well as key steps in executing an intervention.

- For a student bouncing around ideas for choosing a career path, or one who is about to complete his education and embark on a career, this book would serve to open his mind to the possibility of a career in the discipline.

- For business leaders, the book can create awareness for introducing planned change, rather than reacting to events that force the organization to change.

- Of course, anyone with a desire to know more about the subject would benefit from this book as well.

This page is intentionally left blank

How to use this book?

- The book can be used as a guide and reference to understand the role Organizational Development plays in an organization as well as the role that an OD practitioner plays.

- The book is, perhaps, best negotiated with an open mind regarding the possibilities and the paths it could lead to. This is the case because OD is an evolving discipline with new thoughts being added by practitioners.

- It should be read as an introduction to the subject. Should the reader be fascinated by a particular section or chapter, he/she should follow up the reading by looking for more information on the subject of interest.

- For practitioners, the book should also serve as a sounding board and a reality check. Over time, one tends to start building comfort and prejudice in certain areas of a subject over others. The same might happen with OD. Hence, a periodic reference to a tome of this nature will serve to remind practitioners about the vast possibilities and options that the discipline provides for addressing issues in organizations.

This page is intentionally left blank

Chapter **1**

Introduction to an Organization and Organizational Development

This chapter introduces the meaning of an organization, the reasons they are created by humans, their defining characteristics as well as the challenges faced by them in a constantly changing world. Change is a lead-in to the introduction of Organizational Development which leads organizations from reacting to change to controlling their destiny by introducing planned change.

Key learning objectives include the reader's understanding of the following:

- Characteristics of Organizational Development
- The assumptions that underpin the discipline
- Core values of Organizational Development

- What is not Organizational Development, while comparing with disciplines that it sometimes gets confused with

1.1 An Organization

Organizations are an integral and important part of human life. When individuals come together to achieve certain goals by sharing work and acting with understanding over a long period of time, an organization is formed. It is often confused with being a legal entity, generally in the context of a business, but an organization is a much wider term. Two friends planning to climb a mountain peak together and sharing the responsibilities and preparation for it constitutes an organization. A family can be considered one of the primary units of an organization in society. Other units of organizations are larger, formal, and have limited objectives. Here are some of the characteristics of an organization: (Note: While an organization can be any arrangement of people who meet these characteristics, the general reference will be to an organization created for a formal activity like carrying on a business.)

Common goal – The main reason for the existence of an organization is to accomplish some common goal. The structure of the organization is bound by a common goal. Without the glue of a common goal, the parts of the organization are merely individual units and not an organization.

Division of labor – The work that an organization needs to do is done with the help of resources like people, materials, and equipment. People involved are assigned work keeping in mind the optimum output. Different people will be doing different tasks based on their skills and specialization to create optimum output for the organization.

Authority structure – An organization is seeded when a person or a set of people decide to set it up for the attainment of defined goals. In most cases, they will need the support of people working in the organization not only to attain goals but also to expand their footprint. This results in the creation of authority or organizational structure usually under the people who set up the organization. The structure could have multiple levels, with some parts of the goals and work being consolidated at every level, going upwards and ending with the leaders.

Group – It is people who constitute the dynamic elements of an organization and work in groups in various departments of the organization.

Communication – There is a free flow of communication through various official channels among people across various departments. Most of the communication is in written form. Informal methods of communication, sometimes known as grapevine communications, also exist in many organizations and are always oral. However, for important agreements, some form of written communication is usually required.

Coordination – The diverse efforts of functional departments are integrated towards the common objective through a defined process of coordination.

Environment – The environment of an organization is influenced by political, social, legal, and economic factors. It is also influenced by internal factors like capital, level of technology, human resources, and moral and social leanings of individual participants.

Rules and regulations - Every organization is governed by a set of rules and regulations for orderly conduct.

Just like no two individuals are alike, no two organizations are alike in all aspects. Various combinations of organizational characteristics like goals, people, environment, and authority structure result in a unique organizational culture, organizational health, and organizational politics.

Organizational culture is the glue that refers to shared meaning imbibed by the employees that distinguish the organization from other organizations. It is the glue that holds the organization together strongly or weakly depending upon its quality. Organizational culture conveys a sense of identity for its members. It facilitates the generation of something larger than one's self-interest. Many organizations even struggle to define their culture. However, organizational culture exists, develops organically with the organization, and is one of the hardest things to change as the organization gets older.

Organizational health refers to the capacity of an organization to cope with change and continue to function with a high-performing workplace culture designed to meet the goals defined. When employees are happy with their work and careers, organizational health improves.

It will be the endeavor of any organization to become a healthy organization characterized by effective sharing of goals, great teamwork, high employee morale, strong leadership, ability to handle poor performance, good understanding of risks, ability, and agility to adapt to opportunities and challenges and clearly define structure.

1.2 The World Today

"Change is the only constant" is a phrase we hear often, believed to be coined by the Greek philosopher Heraclitus. And we are witness to the impact of change all around us. The world is in constant flux as change has become constant. It is true as much to individuals as it is to organizations.

Organizations are facing unprecedented uncertainty as faster and easier ways of travel and global trade for goods, services, and information flow is making the world a global village. Globalization has altered the market dynamics for organizations. Goods, services, human resources, education, healthcare, and capital are moving across borders and bringing in complexities and uncertainties due to economic interdependence and social differences. They have given rise to gigantic organizations like Apple and Facebook, which would have been unthinkable just a generation back.

An example of economic interdependence leading to chaos is the financial crisis that started with the USA in 2008, spreading across the world and jolting the global economy as a whole. Another example is how the world fretted and perspired when the gigantic container ship Evergreen ran aground for a few days blocking traffic in Suez Canal. The Covid-19 pandemic spread rapidly across the world as a result of the possibility of traveling across the world in a few hours and increasing population and interactions.

Rapid strides in information technology have forced organizations to rethink, redefine and refine traditional business models, their methods of working, and the ways that knowledge is shared and put to use on the whole. This has changed the cost and revenue dynamics of many businesses. Thanks to information technology, new entrepreneurs are springing up in countries where there was very little business activity, thus making it difficult to predict where the competition will come from. With products and services flowing from all over at competitive prices, organizations are under increasing pressure for cost containment.

With markets spread all over the world, organizations have come up with new ways to accelerate and hold on to the market by forming alliances, outsourcing, offshoring, and functioning through virtual offices. Managing these new ways of doing business and rapid course correction is called for in the face of external, political, and economic challenges and increased uncertainties for organizations.

With the advent of modern communication and speedier modes of travel, the world has become a global village with a free flow of information about new developments. Customers and the common public are armed with information and knowledge and have become more demanding of products and services on offer from all types of organizations. The progress in recent years has been so rapid that technologies have shorter life cycles and investors have become more demanding of larger outcomes when they invest their money. The aspirations of employees in organizations have changed with education and exposure, putting pressure on organizations to increase efforts for meaningful engagement.

Whether we like it or not, the theme of "change is the only constant" is here to stay. In fact, change is happening faster and faster all the time, fueled by previous changes and development. The pace of change we have witnessed is expected to look like a crawl in the face of change that is expected to be unleashed in the future. It will be a defining characteristic of this era. As a consequence, organizations that are staid, static, and resistant to change will face challenges. But, with openness to change, the chances of survival and success are expected to increase. Organizations, in order to prosper and grow, need to strive to create and manage change in order to move to a higher performance plane in which employees can grow and develop.

These uncertainties and changes demand managers who are not only flexible and adaptive to change but also able to sense and diagnose problems and manage change to solve the issues.

1.3 What is Organizational Development?

So, if change is happening and threatening us, what is to be done?

Survival being a key instinct, of both humans and organizations, the process of handling challenges has been underway for many decades and has come to be known as the discipline of Organizational Development, or OD. Organizational Development has gradually emerged as a discipline and profession in the decades following World War II.

Organizational Development introduces planned change designed to meet one or more goals of the organization. It is usually managed as a distinct activity separate from the day-to-day operations of the company and follows a designed sequence of steps and processes. It is an interdisciplinary field with components coming from various disciplines. Since it is a field with diverse roots, there are many definitions of Organizational Development and these definitions depend on the emphasis of the practitioner who espoused it. These definitions have also changed over time.

Let us take a look at how various pioneers in the field of Organizational Development have referred to the discipline. As we proceed from older to newer definitions, we can notice how more and more disciplines have been pulled in over the period of time, making OD a vast, interlinked interdisciplinary practice.

Wendell L French referred to OD as a 'long-range effort' designed to improve the organization's ability to solve problems and to handle change occurring in the external environment.[1]

Richard Beckhard (1969) saw organizational development as an organization-wide 'planned effort' that was 'managed from top' for greater effectiveness. Interventions were planned with the help of behavioral sciences."[2]

Warren G Bennis went to the extent of referring to organizational development as an 'educational strategy' that was capable of impacting the culture of an organization with the aim of becoming more receptive to change, such as that introduced through new technologies or through challenges presented by the marketplace and the accelerating rate of such change.[3]

Michael Beer (1980) defined organizational development as a series of steps that started with the process of data collection

---

1. French, Wendell L. 1969. "Organization Development: Objectives, Assumptions and Strategies." *California Management Review 12 23-34*

2. Beckhard, Richard. 1969. "Organization Development: Strategies and Models." (Addison-Wesley)

3. Bennis, Warren G. 1969. "Organization development: Its nature, origin and prospects." (Addison-Wesley)

that was followed by 'diagnosis, action-planning, intervention and evaluation' designed to bring together 'organizational structure, process, strategy, people and culture.' Importantly, it helped in creating the capability of what he called 'self-renewal' in the organization with the help of which it could handle future change. He saw the need for a 'change agent' along with the use of behavioral science theory, research, and technology for the process to be effective.[4]

For Wyatt Warren Burke, organizational development was a 'deliberate process of change' that impacted an organization's culture with the help of 'behavioral science technology, research and theory.'[5]

Warren W. Burke and David L. Bradford referred to organizational development as a 'system-wide process of planned change' which had the clear objective of improving the effectiveness of the organization. They also used the word 'congruence' to define the importance of interplay between the external environment, mission, strategy, leadership, culture, structure, information and reward systems, and work policies and procedures."[6]

From the above definitions, it is clear that Organizational Development involves system-wide **planned change**. Planned change is designed to lead to outcomes that are more in control of the organization as compared to unplanned change that can lead to havoc and uncertainty. These definitions lay emphasis

---

4. Beer, Michael. 1980. "Organization Change and Development: A Systems View." (Goodyear Publishing)

5. Burke, Wyatt Warren. 1982. "Organization Development: Principles and Practices." (Little, Brown)

6. Warren W. Burke, David L. Bradford. 2005. "The Crisis in OD." *Reinventing Organization Development* (John Wiley & Sons)

on the application of knowledge gained through the social and behavioral sciences such as psychology, sociology, business, and management to organizational change. It is to be noted that over a period of time organizations have developed less hierarchical structures and this has resulted in OD activities not necessarily happening at the top management level.

These definitions repeatedly emphasize the following:

- OD focuses on culture and processes

- OD focuses on the human and social side of an organization

- OD relies on the action research model with extensive participation by employees

- OD takes a developmental view that aims at the betterment of both the individual and organization; in other words, a win-win situation

- OD encourages the involvement and participation by all the levels of organization in problem-solving and decision making.

1.4 Characteristics of Organizational Development

From the various definitions of OD, we can glean the following characteristics of OD effort:

It is a planned and long-range initiative

OD is planned change. It is not a quick-fix approach. OD calls for a long-range approach to change systems and attitudes to better the organization's problem-solving and renewal process. It is undertaken in a phased manner and over a long period with the help of a change agent or catalyst who could be an internal expert or an external consultant. It is not a stop-and-start process but continuous as the aim is to create sustainable improvements in organizational effectiveness. Simple assignments could be around 3 to 12 months long while complex assignments might need several years to fulfill set objectives.

It has political implications

The OD effort is centered around the political structure of the organization. The OD effort will be impacted by the hierarchical structure of authority, status differences, and individual power strategy.

OD practitioners foster collaboration and participation which empowers participants. Hence, it is imperative for the OD practitioner to know who makes the decisions, where the vocal and silent political bases are, and who needs to be convinced of the strategies so that he/she buys into them and carries forward the strategies to ensure their success.

An OD intervention could lead to a change in the power structure of an organization. Hence, like all change, it is likely to be uncomfortable. It is important for the leadership to demonstrate its commitment to the initiative and take people into confidence while doing so.

OD is a systematic approach

OD focuses on the total system and its interdependent parts to increase organizational effectiveness. OD seeks resolutions taking into account the internal and external context of the organization. This involves working closely with employees within and stakeholders like customers, investors, and the larger community which could include many others like regulators, vendors, etc.. The focus of OD is not merely to solve a single or temporary issue in an organization; it goes beyond that.

OD relies on well-defined and established processes

Being an interdisciplinary field, OD liberally borrows from other subjects to introduce change in an organization. The change processes adopted by different practitioners could vary. However, most of the processes would cover the following steps:

1. Identifying a need for change

2. Understanding the situation through problem identification and situational assessment

3. Planning interventions and gaining acceptance through action planning

4. Administration of interventions by implementing an intervention, evaluating the outcome of the intervention, and feedback

5. Monitoring and institutionalizing the change

OD is not just anything done to better an organization. It is a particular kind of change process designed to bring about a particular kind of end result. The different steps of organizational development are cyclical in nature beginning with a problem and ending with a sustainable solution and its impact assessment on the system.

If the feedback is found unsatisfactory, the process is repeated. OD is an unfolding and evolving series of events.

It is goal-oriented

OD aligns the organization's systems with people and increases the organizational health and functional abilities of the entire organization. It is tied to specific goals to improve the stability and profitability of the organization and its sustainability in the long run. The final aim of an OD catalyst is to build a set of right attitudes and a suitable action plan for further progress toward its own renewal and development.

It is designed to deliver value

OD effort is guided by values relating to approach and functioning with individuals, teams, and organizations. The core values of the practice of OD are quality of life, empowerment, growth, efficiency, effectiveness, excellence, freedom, responsibility, justice, cooperation, and integration.

It is behavior-oriented

Organizational development uses tools and research findings of behavioral sciences to understand people, systems, and their interactions. It utilizes interventions supported by the knowledge from behavioral sciences to bring about a change in the attitudes and competencies of people.

While deciding the direction of change is crucial, managing employees' personal reactions is important too. A successful OD intervention would result in employees being recognized, involved, and satisfied.

1.5 Assumptions made in Organizational Development

The practice of OD relies on a set of fundamental assumptions regarding the capability, desire, ability, and behavior of organizations and individuals. They can be summarized as follows:

- People react to how they are treated. Better treatment results in better productivity in organizations.

- Work must meet the individual's needs and the organization's needs.

- Most people are motivated by challenging and meaningful work, not controls, threats, and punishment.

- People will exercise self-direction if they are committed to the objectives. They are not lazy.

- Basic building blocks of organizations are groups; therefore, the units of change that OD seeks to introduce are groups.

- Organizations suppress feelings which also leads to the suppression of commitment.

- Groups that learn to work using open and constructive feedback are able to be more productive.

- People work best in supportive and trusting environments. Change is best implemented when people are part of the change process.

- An organization should add up to more than the sum of its members.

- Creativity, ingenuity, and imagination are widely distributed among the population and need a fostering and supportive environment to flower.

- An organization and its members are mutually dependent.

- People want to do great things; individually as well as collectively.

- People have the latent ability to do great things.

- Greatness happens when an environment is created to support it.

1.6 Core Values of OD

OD has always operated with a framework of humanistic and ethical concern for people. Though all OD practitioners might not prescribe to a fixed set of values, and they might not be enshrined anywhere as the unique set of values to be adhered to, most practitioners do not lose sight of the following:

Fairness: It is necessary that people in organizations be treated equitably without discrimination and with dignity.

Human development: It is important for people in organizations to have opportunities for learning and for growth towards a full realization of their capabilities and potential.

Choice: It is important that people in organizations are free from coercion and arbitrary use of authority.

Openness: It is in the interest of the organizations that communications be conducted with honesty, integrity, and forthrightness.

Balance of autonomy and constraint: It is imperative that people in organizations have the autonomy and freedom to perform their work assignments as they see fit.

1.7 What OD is not

When attempting to gain an understanding of a subject, we can also benefit through an effort at gaining an understanding of what the subject is not about.

- OD is not about short-term manipulation to achieve immediate financial gains. OD is an adaptable and real-time discipline that encounters living systems that need feedback to govern their next moves and adjustments. OD is interactive and participative.

- OD is not a micro-approach to change. OD focuses on the macro goals of an organization for an all-encompassing improvement.

- OD is not one single technique. Many different techniques such as sensitivity training, job enrichment, and management training could be used in OD but no single technique can claim to be the representation of the OD discipline.

- OD does not advocate ad hoc or random changes. OD is used in a systematic appraisal and diagnosis of problems, leading to specific types of change efforts.

- OD is not just aimed at improving employee morale or changing attitudes. OD is aimed at overall organizational health and effectiveness.

- There is no one-size-fits-all cookbook approach to OD. Organizations are living systems and they need organic and emerging helping processes for transformation.

The discipline often gets mixed up and confused with Human Resource Management, Change Management, and Organizational Change. This section tries to distinguish OD from these other disciplines.

OD vs. Human Resource Management

HR has developed as a function that seeks to ensure that the organization's people practices are set up and administered so that they contribute to the organization's goals. It is a function that contributes to the goals through its work but does not seek to influence or change the goals. It is often looked upon as an operational function.

OD, on the other hand, has broader coverage, even though a significant part of it may often be related to people-related processes and practices. It looks forward and seeks to bring about change in an organization in order that it is better placed to navigate the currents of the future.

While HR may implement and monitor a performance management system in the organization, OD will have the remit to review and evaluate it and recommend changes, if deemed an improvement. Once that is done, HR will implement the modified performance management system.

OD vs. Change Management

Change management is considered to be the sum total of the processes used by an organization in the implementation and management of change, either brought about internally or as a result of the external environment and forces. It also seeks to ensure that the core business is not derailed as a result of the change implementation. The human processes and implications of change are usually the most critical to be managed.

While both OD and change management are aligned in their usage of plans, processes, and goals, change management usually limits itself to the implementation of change and controlling the negative fallout, if any. OD is considered to be a wider subject with its focus on equipping the organization to initiate as well as manage the change today, as well as in the future. It supports the development of human participation as well as potential.

While all OD will involve some amount of change management, the opposite, of all change management involving OD, is not necessarily true.

OD vs. Organizational Change

Organizational change is perhaps a less frequently used term. Moreover, it is used in generic terms to refer to change, rather than as a technical term that has a specific meaning, like OD.

That being said, organizational change can be said to be a wider term than OD, which has a specific connotation and is hence used only in that context. Organizational development can contribute to organizational change. At the same time, there could be other contributors to organizational change as well.

Quiz

1. An arrangement between people that is not registered cannot be called an organization.

   a. True

   b. False

2. Select which of the following statements are correct (you can choose more than one).

   a. No two individuals are alike

   b. All organizations are alike

   c. All individuals are alike

   d. None of the above

3. Which of the following quotes most closely identify the main reason organizations face challenges:

   a. "Everything that can be invented has been invented"

   b. "Change is the only constant"

   c. "Education is the most powerful weapon which you can use to change the world."

4. **The financial crisis that started with the USA in 2008, spreading across the world and jolting the global economy as a whole, and the Covid-19 pandemic that spread rapidly across the world are examples of:**

    a. Environmental degradation around the world

    b. The global influence of USA

    c. Increasing globalization and interaction across the world

    d. The rising influence of China

5. **Which of the following is not true about Organizational Development?**

    a. Organizational Development is a reaction to change taking place in the environment

    b. It is designed to meet one or more goals of the organization

    c. It is usually managed as a distinct activity, separate from the day-to-day operations of the company

    d. It follows a designed sequence of steps and processes

6. **Which of these are characteristics of OD? (you can choose more than one)**

    a. OD focuses on culture and processes

    b. OD focuses on the material, equipment, and machinery side of an organization

    c. OD relies on the action research model with extensive participation by employees

    d. OD takes a developmental view that aims at the betterment of the organization and not the individual

7. **The change processes adopted by different practitioners would definitely cover which of the following steps (you can choose more than one):**

    a. Identifying a need for change

    b. Understanding the situation through problem identification and situational assessment planning interventions and gaining acceptance

    c. Planning interventions and gaining acceptance through action planning

    d. Administration of interventions by implementing an intervention, evaluating the outcome of the intervention and feedback

    e. Monitoring and institutionalizing the change

8. **Which of the following are incorrect assumptions regarding OD? (you can choose more than one)**

    a. People react to how they are treated. Better treatment results in better productivity in organizations.

    b. Work must meet the individual's needs and the organization's needs.

    c. Most people are motivated by controls, threats, and punishment and not by challenging and meaningful work

    d. People will exercise self-direction if they are committed to the objectives. They are not lazy.

9. **Which of the following are correct assumptions are. OD? (you can choose more than one)**

   a. Basic building blocks of organizations are groups; therefore, the units of change that OD seeks to introduce are groups.

   b. Organizations suppress feelings which also leads to the suppression of commitment.

   c. Groups that learn to work using open and constructive feedback tend to slacken off and become less productive.

   d. Change is best implemented when people are not a part of the change process

10. **Choose the correct statements (You can choose more than one)**

   a. Organizational Development focuses on the organization while Organization Development focuses on people in the organization

   b. Organization Development focuses on the organization while Organizational Development focuses on people in the organization

   c. Both Organization Development and Organization Development can be used interchangeably and mean the same

Answers	1 – b	2 – a	3 – b	4 – c	5 – a
	6 – a, c	7 – all correct	8 – c	9 – a, b	10 – c

Chapter Summary

- ◆ Organizational Development and Organization Development can be used interchangeably

- ◆ An organization is created when individuals come together to achieve common goals

- ◆ The world is changing faster and faster, threatening business models of organizations

- ◆ OD helps in ushering planned change into organizations so that they are equipped to handle the changing environment better

- ◆ OD interventions have common characteristics like being long-term, goal-oriented, designed to deliver value, political and strategic in nature, systematic, and people and behavior-oriented

- ◆ OD is different from Organizational Change, Human Resource Management and Change Management

Chapter 2

The Relevance of Organizational Development

This chapter builds on the concept of OD introduced earlier, develops the goals of OD, and what it seeks to contribute to an organization.

Key learning objectives include the reader's understanding of the following:

- Goals of OD

- Movement from reactive to planned change

- Changes likely to impact organizations profoundly

2.1 Goals of Organizational Development

An organization is an artificial creation. It is created for a specific purpose. A business organization is created for the purpose of creating value for its investors/founders/creators through the conduct of a certain type of business activity.

All activities carried out by such an entity are also deliberate in nature. They are conducted with a definite goal in mind and are never random. Organizational development is no different. The objective of OD is the achievement of defined goals.

While goals could vary from one organization to another, here are a few of the most important goals for organizational development:

Enhancement of profits

Enhancement of profits remains the ultimate goal for all organizations. While a number of ancillary goals have emerged over a period of time, including those related to sustainability, the goal of profit maximization remains the most important one.

OD interventions are geared towards the enhancement of productivity of employees, increasing revenue opportunities, creating processing efficiencies, and product innovations; in general, doing more with less. This is geared towards maximizing the long-term profits of the organization. Short-term profitability could be an erroneous standard. You could make profits one year and losses the next. That is not the goal of OD interventions. The goal is sustained and long-term profit maximization.

Ushering in change and innovation

As discussed earlier, 'change is the only constant' is a theme all organizations need to be aware of. An organization that resists change, risks obsolescence and irrelevance. The world is full of examples of corporations that, from a position of strength in their industries, slid to extinction within a short period of time as they failed to embrace emerging technologies and the change they brought about.

But it is easier said than done. It is a brave organization that will jeopardize its present revenue stream, which seems strong, and instead, choose to invest money in a product that might become popular in the future. Many organizations will prefer to continue with a successful product and wait and watch the future unfold.

OD seeks to create an environment in the organization that constantly seeks validation through involving itself in the marketplace, seeking data, analyzing competition, conducting market research, and listening to customers as well as employees. OD seeks to ingrain a virtuous cycle within the culture of the organization so that it sees value in implementing these processes that lead to change and innovation.

Efficiency and productivity enhancement

A business tracks its performance on a document known as an Income Statement, also known as a Profit and Loss account. The statement records its income on one side and expenses on the other. If income is higher than the expenses, the business gains a profit. If expenses are higher, the difference is a loss to the business.

Many companies have OD interventions to focus their attention on the expense side. What this means is that the effort of the company is to create efficiencies in how resources are consumed in pursuit of revenues. In essence, they try to create efficiency in processing and enhance the productivity of resources such as manpower, real estate, and machinery, so that they can achieve more.

Continuous improvement

In May 1954, Sir Roger Bannister ran the mile in under 4 minutes and was the first man to do so. Hailed as a superhuman achievement, it was expected to be never surpassed. But we know better now. In the eighties, Sebastian Coe and Steve Ovett were going head to head and running the mile in under 3 minutes and 50 seconds. The record has, since, gone under 3 minutes 40 seconds.

In tennis, as per data available from Grand Slam events, the average speed of the first serve was less than 170 km per hour, till the early nineties. That average had increased to 180 km per hour by the end of the first decade of the 2000s. Most of the fastest serves recorded belong to the post-2000 era.

Wherever you look, there is improvement. These examples of human endeavor in sport, and pushing of boundaries amply demonstrate the point. Striving for the better in a way defines human existence. Business is no different. Everyone is trying to do better and better all the time. Staying with yesterday's quality is just not good enough anymore. You have to do more.

Continuous improvement is not a choice. It is a survival strategy. And OD practitioners are helping organizations imbibe it as a core part of their being and existence.

Development of employees

Unlike material resources, such as machines, raw materials, etc., human resources need to be handled with care and sensitivity. The treatment of employees and how well they are allowed to contribute often makes or breaks a business.

Just as the organization, employees also confront changes. At times, their jobs become redundant because of automation. Demand for newer skills increases while older skills gradually fade out. In a fast-changing world, OD helps employees adapt and keep pace with changing times and stay relevant. It could even be as simple as working on communication channels within the organization so that employees feel engaged and aligned with its goals and mission.

From the perspective of employees, the major objectives of OD interventions would be:

- Making employees aware of the mission and goals of the organization which could be expected to lead to better engagement and ownership

- Encouraging and instilling a problem-solving approach instead of passing the buck

- Creation of an environment where participation is encouraged and feedback is valued; participation in planning is understood to be a building block for ownership

- Reducing the dependence on formal lines of authority based on designation and encouraging skill and knowledge-based contribution.

- Managing interpersonal conflict.

- Creation of an environment where people trust each other and feel valued, and preparing individuals to embrace change.

Case Study – Reducing staff attrition by providing training and development and creating engagement

1. A Life Insurance company faced the issue of agent attrition, a common problem for companies with a large entry-level sales force. After a detailed study on reasons and patterns by OD experts, it was decided that one of the contributors to the attrition was a belief that the company was not interested in their career and growth. It was only interested in getting them to work so that it could make money.

2. A training and development plan, over and above job-related training, was created to address the issue and demonstrate the company's commitment to them.

3. The attrition for a team was 5% per month for a 12-month period.

4. In the same period, 400 members of the team got an opportunity to attend various training programs arranged by the company.

5. At the normal team rate of attrition of 5% per month, 20 out of these 400 would have attrited every month. Or 240 people in the whole year.

6. However, the actual rate of attrition from this group at the end of the year was 1.88% per month or 7.5 people per month. Or 90 for the whole year.

7. Thus, resulting in a saving of 150 people in the entire year. The savings in the form of hiring and training new hires far exceeded the cost incurred on the training programs.

8. Why did this happen?

9. The belief is that investment in training makes an employee feel wanted and that the company is interested in their development and growth.

2.2 From Reacting to Change to Planned Change

Human beings, and the institutions created by them, such as organizations, have an inbuilt safety mechanism that is designed to ferret out ways of safety and prosperity. If we are in a building and an earthquake strikes in the area, our immediate response is to rush out to the safety of open ground. If we see an object hurled at us, we instinctively take evasive action or prepare to block it before it hits us.

Organizations are no different. Though it does not have a mind of its own, the collective minds of the people managing the organization act in a similar manner. Once set up with certain goals in mind, the organization's objective and effort seek the best path toward those defined goals. Naturally, it also encounters several obstacles along the way, such as competition, changes in rules, or the inability to hire the right people. Again, the collective wisdom of the management seeks to thread a path around those hurdles in order to keep it moving towards its goals.

Of course, as we perhaps know, human efforts don't always succeed. Some people perish in earthquakes if they are unable to take action in time or are in a situation where they cannot. Sometimes we get hit by the projectile hurled at us. Organizations also fail. Unable to find a way towards the intended goals, some shut down. Many others struggle, alternating between success and failure.

While results may not always work out in our favor, the effort is always designed to keep us safe and prosperous, including the organizations we manage. Organizations must keep looking out for threats that emerge on the horizon and keep adapting to the economic, political, and technological changes that could derail their mission. At times, it may even need to look into the future and change its strategic direction. It is now a commonly accepted belief that the change that will be unleashed in the future will be far greater than anything we have experienced so far.

And, in the interest of continued relevance, it will need to be managed.

The need for organizations to constantly look out for signs of trouble and keep finding responses to the changes taking place led to the emergence of the discipline of Organizational development (OD).

What are some of the changes taking place in the world that are likely to impact organizations profoundly?

Globalization

The world is becoming smaller and smaller. Goods and people are able to move freely around the world. If Sony launched a new model of the Sony Walkman in Japan in the eighties, many nations around the world would not even hear of it till many months later. Today, if Apple introduces a new model of the iPhone, it is available on the same day in Pakistan and Kenya, as it is in the US. A person of Indian origin is the CEO of Google, one of the most admired companies in the world, while Australian Peter Kaliaropoulos was the CEO of Starhub, one of the largest telecom companies in Singapore, till a few months back.

Despite efforts by some nations at protectionism, promoting their own products and people, and creating barriers against the entry of foreign goods and resources, it seems like an irreversible trend.

What does globalization mean to organizations?

For one, the competition is no longer local, it is global. You are no longer competing against locally produced goods and services. Supply chain and logistics companies make it possible for goods to be available anywhere in the world. Hence, the best quality, at the right price point, will find acceptance while inferior quality will not. Hence, putting two and two together, good quality will benefit while poor quality will suffer. Consumers, hopefully, will be able to access the best quality from anywhere in the world.

However, there is no unmixed blessing. The downside of this is that challenges faced in one part of the world could easily spread to others. The subprime mortgage initiated the financial crisis of the United States in 2007–2008 spreading around the world, creating a global recession, and impacting economies in almost every region of the world.

There are other challenges too. Just as the distribution of a product is possible around the world, the search for resources and input materials can also be done anywhere in the world. Accessing and consuming natural resources from far-away locations seems to have created a lack of responsibility with environmental regulations not being very tight in many parts of the world and bringing us all to the brink of an environmental catastrophe.

That being said, globalization is an irreversible trend. We will need to find ways to address the issues it creates, rather than put a stop to it.

Technology

Who is not witness to the transformative power of technology, especially the revolution that has taken place in digital technologies during the lifetime of many of us?

Google, Facebook, Amazon, Apple, and Tesla are household names today. The rapidly expanding reach of telecommunications and the internet has revolutionized access to information in the darkest corners of the world. The same information is available to users around the world at the click of a button at the same time. Businesses based on information asymmetry are a thing of the past.

The business world is also full of examples of companies that occupied a leadership position in their industry but faded out within just a few years as they failed to embrace new and emerging technologies in time.

Technology is making it possible for work to be done from far away. This has given rise to the Business Process Outsourcing (BPO) industry. Data entry for a credit card sold in the UK is probably being done somewhere in the Philippines. This has given a huge cost advantage to companies that have the scale to offshore work to cheaper locations. At the same time, it has managed to create work opportunities in the less economically developed parts of the world, serving to play the economic bridge in bringing the two ends closer to each other.

Wherever you look, technology-driven innovations are taking place. E-commerce has revolutionized the way we shop. E-learning is delivering information and knowledge more cost-effectively than ever before to interested learners. Social media has changed the way people interact and converse and take trends global. Cloud computing has freed work from a locational limitation. The emergence of 'work from home,' a trend that gathered steam during the pandemic-induced lockdowns, is supported by technology.

People

As we have seen, people adapt to changing circumstances in an effort to survive and thrive. This reflex action also rubs off on organizations that may have been created for a specific purpose, but are run and managed by people.

While there are a wide variety of people involved in any large corporation in many different capacities, one way of classifying them is whether they have a managerial role where they influence, guide, and manage others, or a role as an individual contributor where one is responsible for one's own contribution to the company.

Both roles have undergone a transformation and, no doubt will continue to see more of it. The transformation has been in response to the changes happening in the environment, including in globalization and technology, as well as independent of them.

An organization that does everything on its own has been consigned to the pages of history. Cooperation, networking, and alliances are ways in which organizations that have similar goals collaborate and try to stand out from the crowd. While there has always been a reliance on vendors and partners for procurement of parts as well as distribution of output, the alliances that are emerging are now more strategic in nature. It is recognized that there are many smart people and many smart organizations in the world and that one person or organization cannot be the best at everything. Hence, the openness and willingness to tap into the expertise of others is creating new products as well as opportunities.

It used to be a matter of pride for organizations to be growing in size in terms of parameters like the number of employees, number of offices, and number of countries served, apart from financial parameters which always remain relevant. Today's organization is more aware of the challenges size could bring and is focused on doing more with less. It is expected to be easier to navigate a lean ship through troubled waters as compared to an overladen ship that could lurch dangerously when buffeted by strong winds and rough seas, as all organizations encounter from time to time.

A growing complement of leaders is recognizing that they also need to give back in equal measure to the society that has enabled them to prosper. Environment, Sustainability, and Governance (ESG) is now on the agenda of many forward-looking organizations. OD practitioners are helping organizations change proactively and have more control over their destinies rather than merely reacting in hindsight.

Employees and workers are also changing. A few decades back, the equation was loaded in favor of the employer. Employee-employer dynamics are undergoing change. Employees are becoming more discerning in their choice of employer. Many people would prefer to be counted as an employee of a company that contributes to the ESG effort. These preferences are also driving organizational behavior as they need to continue to attract talent for survival and growth.

While these may be the major ones, there are many other changes that are happening every moment. The question to ask at this point is: How are organizations handling this change?

Through Organizational Development, of course.

With the support of OD practitioners, organizations are not merely reacting to change, they are proactively engaging in it and managing it in an effort to better control the outcomes. These practitioners are helping leaders as well as workers understand the impact of change and equipping them to handle it. This effort is not limited to business corporations. Government agencies, non-profits, educational institutions, and everyone is recognizing the need and introducing OD as a discipline. OD is helping everyone who works in an organization manage change better.

Quiz

1. **Select the statements that correctly describe an organization (you can choose more than one)**

   a. An organization is a natural creation.

   b. An organization is created for a specific purpose.

   c. An organization is created for the purpose of destroying value for its investors/founders/creators.

   d. An organization has permanent existence.

2. **Which of the following is not a major goal of OD interventions? (you can choose more than one)**

   a. Profit enhancement

   b. Continuous improvement

   c. Employee development

   d. Real estate price escalation

3. **The 'enhancement of profit' goal of an organization is geared towards short-term profit enhancement and not long-term profit.**

   a. True

   b. False

4. Income (or Revenue) and Expense are two sides of an Income Statement. OD interventions launched by organizations operate on which of the two?

   a. Only Income

   b. Only Expense

   c. Could be either, depending on the need

   d. Neither Income nor Expense

5. The main goal of OD interventions that work on the expense side of an Income Statement is:

   a. Reduction of total cost

   b. Increasing total cost

   c. Enhancement of efficiency in resource consumption

   d. Reducing headcount

6. If the world record for a particular race has been getting better over time, in the context of OD, it is an example of

   a. Better training methods

   b. Improved equipment available to athletes

   c. Man's desire for continuous improvement

   d. Man's desire for an easy life

7. **From the perspective of employees, which of the following could be classified as major objectives of OD interventions? (you can choose more than one)**

   a. Making employees aware of the mission and goals of the organization which could be expected to lead to better engagement and ownership

   b. Encouraging and instilling a problem-solving approach instead of passing the buck

   c. Creation of an environment where participation is encouraged and feedback valued; participation in planning is understood to be a building block for ownership

   d. Removing the bottom 20% performers every year

8. **From the perspective of employees, which of the following would not be major objectives of OD interventions? (you can choose more than one)**

   a. Reducing the salary of employees

   b. Reducing the dependence on formal lines of authority based on designation and encouraging skill and knowledge-based contribution.

   c. Managing interpersonal conflict.

   d. Creation of an environment where people trust each other and feel valued, and preparing individuals to embrace change.

9. **Which of the following would we witness in an environment in which competition is global? (you can choose more than one)**

   a. Good quality producers will benefit

   b. Good quality producers will lose

   c. Nothing will change

10. **Environment, Sustainability, and Governance (ESG) is now on the agenda of many forward-looking organizations**

    a. True

    b. False

Answers	1 – b	2 – d	3 – b	4 – c	5 – c
	6 – c	7 – a, b, c	8 – a	9 – a, b	10 – a

Chapter Summary

◆ OD interventions seek to deliver enhanced profits, change and innovation, productivity enhancement, continuous improvement, and development of employees in an organization

◆ It leads the organization from being reactive to change to ushering in planned change

◆ Globalization, technology development, and people are the sources of the biggest changes that organizations face and need to manage

Chapter 3

Evolution and Growth of Organizational Development

This chapter introduces the giants who have contributed to the development of the discipline, traces the path of the streams along which it has developed, and introduces the established models of planned change.

Key learning objectives include the reader's understanding of the following:

- Overview of the pioneers of the discipline

- Knowing about the streams along which OD has developed

- Introduction to various models of planned change that have been developed and used by the pioneers

- The 'general model of planned change' in ensuing chapters

3.1 Pioneers of OD

There is no specific launch date when Organizational Development came into existence. Nobody set out to create a new field called OD. People were simply trying to do their jobs better and creating processes and support systems as they went along. Most of the early names associated with the field of OD were psychologists. In course of time, however, as the practice interfaced with other disciplines, there were contributions from many other fields of study such as anthropology, economics, quality management and continuous improvement, and system theory.

Let us look at some people whose work was instrumental in the establishment of the field of OD as it is practiced today:

Kurt Lewin (mid-1940s)

Though the term OD did not exist during his time, Lewin could be called the "founding father of OD." Lewin created the concepts of force field analysis, sensitivity training leading to team building, feedback, change theory, action research, and self-managed teams.

Richard Beckhard (mid-1960s)

He was a pioneer in advocating changes in a systematic manner across large organizations. Working with Douglas McGregor, Beckhard came up with the theory termed Formula Change. He could be the one who initially coined the term Organizational Development which is widely used now.

W Edwards Deming (1950s Japan, 1980s USA)

He championed continuous process improvement with emphasis on processes arguing that best processes led to best results. Deming is also considered to be one of the early influencers on the discipline known as Quality Management today.

Ron Lippit (late 1940s)

He is recognized as one of the founders of group dynamics and T-groups. Lippit, a pioneer in the development of experimental social psychology was renowned for his work on leadership in small groups and work on planned change. He advocated the seven-step theory of change based on the concept of external agents as catalysts of change.

Carl Rogers (1950s and 1960s)

He was a humanist psychologist who contributed to factors needed for an individual to grow in an organization. He also contributed to the field of behavioral psychology with his approach to counseling with new techniques.

Eric Trust (1950s)

He worked in the UK and is credited with the development of the sociotechnical system (STS) in his work in the coal mines of England. STS focused on the interface among people, machines, and the environment.

3.2 Streams of Evolution

The science of OD has at least four important themes as it started developing half a century ago.

OD has evolved over a period of time expanding and incorporating various disciplines as can be surmised from the subtle but changing emphasis of various definitions of OD by leading practitioners. A detailed analysis of the evolution of OD indicates OD as current practice having emerged from four major backgrounds or stems or paths over a little over half a century.

The Laboratory Training stream

Laboratory training is about learning from a person's "here and now" experience as a member of an ongoing training group. Laboratory training was conducted with strangers as group members. It was also conducted with groups formed by members from different organizations and backgrounds. Such groups met without any specific agenda. Group interactions brought forth to the surface problems of status, communication, self-serving behavior, structure, and leadership. The participants could learn speaking, listening, and how to be effective group members. But experiences learned in the lab training could not be transferred to actual situations at home or elsewhere due to differences in culture, protected and relatively safe environment of laboratory groups, and give-and-take attitudes being different. The failure of laboratory training methods led to training groups within organizations. This led to the emergence of team building.

Action Research and Survey Feedback stream

Studies conducted by social scientists in 1946 form the basis of action research and survey feedback streams. It was discovered that research needed to be closely linked to action if organization members were to use it to manage change. Research data about an organization's functioning was collected through a collaborative effort, and analyzed to find causes of problems based on which solutions were devised and implemented. Further data was collected to assess results and the cycle of data collection and action often continued. The outcome of action research was twofold: members of the organization were able to use research on themselves to guide action and change and social scientists were able to study that process to derive new knowledge that could be used elsewhere. Some of the pioneering action research studies were the work of Lewin and his students at Harwood Manufacturing Company, Whyte and Edith Hamilton's study of Chicago's Tremont Hotel, and Likert and Floyd Mann's study of employee attitudes in Detroit Edison through a company-wide survey. Lester Coch and John French conducted action research studies on overcoming resistance to change leading to the development of participative management as a means of employees being involved in planning and managing change.[7]

Normative Approaches stream

This stream follows from the normative belief that a human relations approach represents "one best" way to manage an organization.

---

7. French, L. Coch and J. 1948. "Overcoming resistance to Change." *Human Relations 1*, 512-32

Of the two leading works in this stream, the first is Likert's Participative Management program which postulates four types of management systems:[8]

1. Exploitive authoritative systems (System 1) exhibit an autocratic approach to leadership leading to mediocre performance.

2. Benevolent authoritative systems (System 2) are similar to System 1 except management is more paternalistic.

3. Consultative systems (System 3) increase employee interaction, communication, and decision-making with management taking the final decisions. This results in higher levels of satisfaction for employees and improved productivity.

At the other end of the scale (from System 1) are systems known as participative group systems which are classified as system 4. Productivity and employee satisfaction is highest in this and is believed to be the result of a linkage of decision-making throughout the system. Through a survey feedback process among group members in organizations, Likert generated action plans to move organizations.

Blake and Mouton's Grid Organizational Development came up with a nine-by-nine grid with concern for production and concern for people being the two axes, and each being scored from 1 to 9. A 9.9 score on the grid was identified as the most effective.[9]

---

8. Likert, R. 1969. The Human Organization. New York: McGraw-Hill

9. R. Blake, J. Mouton. 1964. The Managerial Grid. Houston: Gulf

Productivity and Quality-of-work-life stream

This stem is also called 'sociotechnical systems.' Quality-of-work-life (QWL) programs were the outcome of the research of Eric Trist and colleagues at Tavistock Institute of Human relations in London in the 1960s. QWL programs involved joint participation by unions and management in the design of work. QWL programs led to the discovery of self-managing work groups as a form of work design. QWL migrated to the United States in the 1960s and stayed on till the 1970s. The second phase of QWL started in the USA in 1979 due to the intense growing international competition faced by the United States at home and abroad, especially from Japan with low-cost and high-quality products. QWL programs expanded beyond their initial focus on work design resulting in large-scale and long-term projects including work on organizational efficiency. This second phase of QWL is continuing in the form of "employee involvement" as well as total quality management and six sigma programs.

Other streams such as the 'strategic change' stream have been suggested by some scholars as suitable for addition to the various streams mentioned above. In due course, they will probably join the pantheon as support from scholars grows. For the purpose of this book, we will use the four streams mentioned in this chapter.

3.3 Models of planned Organizational Change

At some stage, one needs to answer the question: How should I do it? Or How is it to be done?

In a scenario where the interplay of technology, information, cross-border competition, new alliances, and virtual organizations make it a complex environment, the ability to manage change successfully sets apart an effective organization from the rest of the crowd. OD is about learning and improving in ways that make individuals, groups and organizations manage change in the future through the process of planned change. By applying behavioral science knowledge in the process of planned change, OD increases the capacity of the organization as a whole to change and improve its functioning and performance.

There are several models, or methods, successfully used by OD practitioners to introduce planned change and enhance the capacity of organizations and people to manage future change.

Action Research model

The classic action research model focuses on planned change as a cyclical process where initial research about the organization provides information to guide subsequent action. Thereafter, the results of the action are assessed to provide further information to guide further action and so on. It is an iterative cycle and multiple rounds may be needed before the organization is able to reach close to the desired outcomes. The greater the support received by the OD experts from the organizational team members, the better the outcomes can be expected to be. It places high emphasis on data gathering and diagnosis prior to action planning and implementation as well as careful evaluation of results after the action is taken.

The concept of the **Action Research model** is attributed to Kurt Lewin. Action research assumes that organizational problems can be solved with cycles of knowledge gathering, implementation of action solutions, and when these dual activities are concurrently and actively practiced by the organization's members. This is expected to contribute to the organization's repository of knowledge.

The various steps in Action research in planned change could be defined as:

1. **Problem definition:** This begins when a person with power and influence in the organization senses one or more problems that could be solved with the help of an OD practitioner.

2. **Consultation with a behavioral (OD) expert:** At this stage, the organization and the OD consultant assess each other carefully. The OD practitioner comes with his own normative, developmental theory or framework of reference with its assumptions and values. Sharing them with the client in the beginning, helps to establish an open and collaborative working environment.

3. **Data gathering and preliminary diagnosis:** This step is usually completed by the OD consultant in collaboration with the organization's members. The four methods of gathering data generally used are interviews, administration of questionnaires, close observation of processes in the organization, and data on organization performance. The sequence is generally that of process observation followed by a semi-structured interview followed by the questionnaire.

4. **Feedback:** The diagnostic data is given as feedback, usually in a group or work-team meetings. The feedback helps members evaluate the strengths and weaknesses of the organization. The consultant provides the client with all the

relevant data for the purpose. Experienced consultants are expected to take care to ensure confidentiality of the source of information if it is needed. They are also expected to ensure that the feedback data is worded appropriately and does not make the client overly defensive.

5. **Joint diagnosis of the problem:** At this stage, members discuss and explore along with the OD consultant whether they would want to work on the identified problems. A close relationship exists between data gathering, diagnosis, and feedback because the consultant summarizes the basic data obtained from the organization's members and presents it back to them for validation and further diagnosis. This is a crucial stage as OD experts and employees working in their own silos do not produce good results in an OD intervention. This is the stage at which the two should be starting to operate in unison by establishing a common TOR (terms of reference) for the initiative. The initiative might be led by the expert but needs to be agreed upon by the organization's members before moving further.

6. **Joint action planning:** At this stage, the OD expert and the client members jointly agree upon further actions to be taken. This is the process of organizational change as the organization decides how best to reach a different stage of quasi-stationary equilibrium. Time and expense of intervention, culture, technology, and environment of the organization come into play while deciding upon specific actions to be taken.

7. **Action:** This is when the change actually gets implemented. Such action cannot be implemented immediately and usually requires a transition period as the organization

moves from the present equilibrium to a desired future state equilibrium.

8. **Data gathering after action:** Action research is a cyclical process. Data must be gathered after action has been taken to measure and determine the effects of the action and to provide the results back to the organization. This may lead to renewed cycles of diagnosis and new action.

This cycle continues till the desired sustainable level of organizational change has been achieved.

Lewin's three-step model

The three-step model of change was proposed by Kurt Lewin as one of the four interrelated elements that comprised his planned approach to change with the other three being field theory, action research, and group dynamics.

This is the oldest OD planned change model. Lewin argued that change is a dynamic process and an ongoing struggle between a set of opposing forces: one pushing in the direction of change called the driving forces and the other pulling in the opposite direction called restraining forces. The struggle between the two sets of forces is portrayed as a force field where a stable situation consists of a state of equilibrium between the two sets of forces. OD practitioners help organization members to identify these forces in the change management process.

The three steps of the model are:

1. **Unfreezing (destabilizing) the status quo position –** This can be achieved either by reducing the strength of restraining forces and/or increasing the driving forces.

The direction of the forces can also be changed so that a restrain can become a push factor. The focus in this stage is to create motivation for change. Individuals are encouraged to replace behaviors and attitudes and it is imperative that people are or become dissatisfied with the old ways of doing things.

2. **Moving to a new situation (changing the current situation and moving towards desired end state**) – This step shifts the behavior of the organization, department, or individual to a different equilibrium or steady state. It involves intervening in the system to develop new behaviors, values, and attitudes through a change in the organizational structure and processes. It has been found that certain activities are necessary to implement the first two stages of the change project. These include disconfirming the validity of the status quo and persuading employees to agree that the existing situation is not beneficial to them. It is also necessary to induce guilt about the existing situation and actively engage employees and leaders in identifying problems and solutions in the unfreezing and moving stages.

   Research has shown that change has to happen quickly to be effective. Organizations that build up change gradually do less well than the ones that get through the movement stage quickly.

3. **Refreezing** – This stage stabilizes the organization at a new state of equilibrium. It is frequently established through the supporting mechanisms that reinforce the organizational state such as organizational culture, rewards, and structures.

Kotter's eight-step model

Some practitioners consider Lewin's three-step model to be too broad to apply in some situations. A number of experts worked on the model in detail to fill up the gaps. The updated version emerged as Kotter's eight-step model, an elaborate one filling the gaps in Lewin's three-step model.

The eight steps of organizational change are:

1. Create a sense of urgency by initiating an open and honest dialogue about the urgent need to change. It involves establishing a sense of urgency by examining reality, possible crises and/or opportunities.

2. Create a guiding coalition of leaders and managers who will work with the rest of the members of the organization and the change agents.

3. Develop and articulate a vision and strategy to direct the change and achieve the goals.

4. Communicate the change to every member in a constant mode. This is to be done not only by emails and flyers but by really acting in a way that communicates the message through actions.

5. Empower broad-based action and act according to the vision by demonstrating the overcoming of obstacles, and encouraging creativity and risk-taking.

6. Create visible short-term wins and allow a reward for those who drive the change. There is a sort of learning process involved which equips the organization to update and learn from the change driving itself.

7. Consolidate gains and build a perspective for future change by promoting and encouraging the people as well as making credible the new systems and practices.

8. Institutionalize the new approach, and develop the leadership by anchoring the new process in the culture of the organization.

Positive model / Appreciative Inquiry model

Both Lewin's model and the Action research model attempt to solve problem areas and are deficit-based approaches. The Positive model is different and focuses on what the organization is doing right. This approach helps members to understand their organization when it is working at its best and build off their capabilities to achieve even better results. Research expectation effects support this model of planned change. It shows that people tend to act in ways that lead to their expectations being realized. This could be seen as a form of a 'visualization' process. Once people are able to visualize a better future, they are also enthused in working towards it.

This process of 'visualization' is implemented through a process known as 'Appreciative Inquiry' (AI) which seeks to infuse a sense of positivity towards the ongoing change. AI is based on social constructionism which assumes that organization members' shared experiences and interactions influence how they perceive the organization and behave in it. AI encourages a positive orientation to how change is conceived and managed. It promotes broad member involvement in creating a shared vision of the organization's positive potential.

The steps in the Positive model approach of planned change are:

Initiate the inquiry: Through a collaborative effort, members determine the subject of change which will be the one they have the most energy to address. It will be a positive subject like increasing customer satisfaction (not reducing customer dissatisfaction) or promoting successful female–male collaboration (not reducing sexual harassment at work).

Inquire into best practices: This involves gathering information about the 'best of what is' in the organization. If the topic is process innovation, the members develop an interview protocol on how new processes were developed and implemented in the organization. The interviews are conducted by organization members; they interview each other and tell stories of new process developments in which they have personally been involved. The stories are put together to form a pool of information describing the organization as innovative.

Discover themes: In this phase, members examine stories to arrive at a set of themes representing common dimensions of members' expectations. The stories of new process development could contain themes about how coworkers came together to support an altered process idea, the flexibility managers gave to the members to work out new processes, and how a visit to a customer sparked a new process idea. It is imperative that all of the underlying mechanisms that helped to generate and support the themes be described. The themes represent the basis for moving from 'what is' to 'what could be.'

Envision a preferred future: Members examine the identified themes, challenge the status quo, and describe a compelling future. They develop statements that bridge the organization's current best practices with ideal possibilities for future organizing.

The propositions should present a truly exciting, provocative, and possible picture of the future. Based on these possibilities, members identify relevant stakeholders and critical organizational processes that must be aligned to support the emergence of the envisioned future. This vision becomes a statement of 'what should be.'

Design and deliver ways to create the future: This phase describes the activities and creates the plans necessary to bring about the vision. This goes into an iterative mode with members making changes, assessing results, and making necessary adjustments as they move the organization towards the vision and sustain 'what will be.'

Critical Research model

The Critical Research model assumes that every organization or group has an ideology, a consistent rationale, about how decisions should be made, how resources should be used, how people should be managed, and how the organization should respond to the environment in which it functions.

A natural tension develops between what people believe should happen and what they believe is actually happening. The basic thrust of a critical research approach to planned change is to identify this discrepancy and use it to power change. Critical research heightens the tension by pointing out the inconsistency.

Critical research views conflict between ideology and actual practices as constructive, leading to self-examination and change. Beckhard's confrontation meetings which bring together two conflicting groups to discuss their differences and to arrive at ways of working together more effectively are close to the critical action approach.

Burke-Litwin model of organizational change

This is an open system model developed by Warne Burke and George Litwin. This model shows how to create first-order change and second-order change called transactional and transformational change respectively.[10]

In the first-order change, some features of the organization change but the fundamental nature of the organization remains the same. In the second-order change, the nature of the organization is fundamentally and substantially altered and the organization is transformed.

The model distinguishes between organizational climate and organizational culture. Organizational climate is defined as the perception of organization members towards the work environment – is it a good place or average place to work, friendly, indifferent or unfriendly, hard-working or easy-going, and so on. These perceptions are relatively easy to change because they are built on organization members' reactions to current managerial and organizational practices. On the other hand, organizational culture is defined as deep-rooted assumptions, values, and beliefs that are enduring, often exist at a subconscious level, and are difficult to change.

The premise of the Burke-Litwin model is that second-order change is the result of addressing leadership, strategy, and mission while first-order change can be brought about by

---

10. Burke, W. W., & Litwin, G. H. 1992. "A casual model of organizational performance and change." Journal of Management 18(3) 523-545

directing attention toward processes, practices, and structures. The model makes a distinction between transactional and transformational leadership. The two concepts came from leadership research which found that some leaders are capable of obtaining extraordinary performance from followers while other leaders are not. Transformational leadership embodies inspiration which leads to new heights of performance. Transactional leadership embodies a fair exchange between leader and follower which leads to normal performance. Transactional leadership is sufficient for first-order change. Transformational leadership is required for causing second-order change.

General Model of Planned change

This framework describes the general framework for planned change. The underlying need for this 'general' model is a model that could be applied and used by a large number of practitioners of OD. Each of the models described earlier has been developed based on certain needs and requirements and is suitable based on the circumstances of the situation. They could also cause some confusion amongst practitioners in terms of their applicability. The General model is a set of systematic steps, based on data and research that should mean the same thing to all people.

The number of steps might vary from one practitioner to another but the underlying principles remain the same, as demonstrated by this illustration.

| Figure 3.1 | General Model of Planned change |

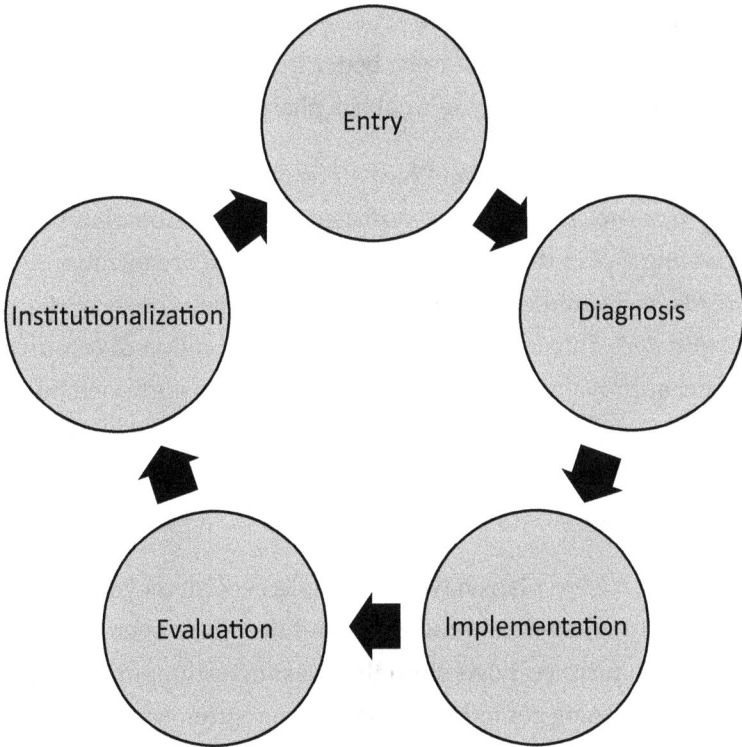

Entry – The starting point is the identification of needs. This is usually left to the discretion of the leaders who, by virtue of their position and role, are expected to have an understanding of what is going right and what is not. Of course, there are many tools and analyses like financial MIS, customer surveys, and employee feedback that they can rely on to identify the organization's need for introducing change or improvement. If they are good enough to lead the organization, they should be good enough to have an understanding of the need for improvement.

Diagnosis – Once a need has been identified, the natural next step is to find out, or investigate the reasons why it is the way it is. This phase provides an understanding of the challenges and barriers that might lie in the path to improvement. Have any attempts been made in the past to address the issue? If yes, what was the outcome? Fresh data could be collected through surveys and data analysis to understand the issue better from different perspectives. This phase is also called the Analysis phase by some.

Implementation (or Action Plan) – The objective of the exercise being to create change, the next phase involves action planning, or creating a plan that would be able to take the organization towards its desired goal as envisioned when the process of change was initiated. This is the stage at which identification of resources is done, approvals obtained, and responsibilities portioned out amongst the team members driving the change. Equally important is the setting up of goals and parameters through which its achievement, or lack of it, could be measured.

Evaluation – After plans have been implemented, they need to be evaluated to understand how successful they have been in driving towards the planned goals since that was the entire purpose of the exercise. There could be a variety of measures, some being collected over a period of time.

Institutionalization – Once it has been established that the implementation has been successful and it is delivering the desired results, an effort needs to be made to institutionalize the process. What this usually means is transitioning the responsibility from a core or project team to the people who run the operations on a day-to-day basis, or BAU (Business as Usual) mode.

Some people consider this phase to be outside the model, as they believe that the first four phases may need to be repeated a number of times till success is achieved. The model is flexible and open to adaptation, as stated at the beginning. Some also like to make a distinction between the Action Planning phase and the Implementation phase, with Implementation starting after the Action Plan has been created.

OD having drawn liberally from other disciplines has been mentioned in the early parts of this book. The General model represents an example of a principle that is widely used in the Quality management function in organizations. It closely resembles a data-driven cycle of improvement referred to as DMAIC (Define—Measure—Analyze—Improve—Control) that quality practitioners are particularly fond of.

The ensuing pages will shed light on each of the steps in the General model.

Quiz

1. The modern discipline of Organizational Development (OD) came into being on:

   a. February 1, 1946

   b. March 5, 1935

   c. August 23, 1962

   d. No definite date

2. The epithet of 'founding father of OD' is most commonly applied to

   a. Richard Beckhard

   b. Kurt Lewin

   c. Ron Lippit

   d. Warren Bennis

3. Who is credited with first coining the term Organizational Development to refer to the discipline?

   a. Edward Demming

   b. Wendell L. French

   c. Wyatt Warren Burke

   d. Richard Beckhard

   e. Richard A. Schnuk

4. **Along which of the following streams did the OD discipline develop?**

   a. Laboratory Training stream

   b. Scientific Enquiry stream

   c. Normative Approaches stream

   d. Productivity and Quality-of-work-life stream

5. **The eight-step model of change was introduced by**

   a. Carl Rogers

   b. Lewin

   c. Kotter

   d. Burke-Litwin

6. **The two axes on Blake and Mouton's Grid Organizational Development are**

   a. Concern for profits

   b. Concern for production

   c. Concern for competition

   d. Concern for people

7. **Which of the following is not a part of Lewin's three-step model?**

   a. Unfreezing (destabilizing) the status quo position

   b. Analyzing (Reviewing) to identify solutions

   c. Moving to a new situation (changing current situation and moving towards desired end state)

   d. Refreezing (stabilizing the organization at a new state of equilibrium)

8. **The Normative Approaches stream follows the normative belief that**

   a. a production-focused approach represents "one best" way to manage an organization.

   b. a human relations approach represents "one best" way to manage an organization.

   c. a profit-driven approach represents "one best" way to manage an organization.

   d. a society-driven approach represents "one best" way to manage an organization.

9. **Which of the following is not a management system proposed by Libert in his Participative Management program?**

    a. Exploitive authoritative systems

    b. Benevolent authoritative systems

    c. Consultative systems

    d. Participative group systems

    e. None of the above

10. **In the General Model of Planned Change, the sequence followed is:**

    a. Entry – Institutionalization – Diagnosis – Implementation – Evaluation

    b. Entry – Evaluation – Institutionalization – Implementation – Diagnosis

    c. Entry – Diagnosis – Implementation – Evaluation - Institutionalization

    d. Diagnosis – Implementation – Evaluation – Institutionalization – Entry

Answers	1 – d	2 – b	3 – d	4 – a, c, d	5 – c
	6 – b, d	7 – b	8 – b	9 – e	10 – c

Chapter Summary

◆ A series of early contributors have helped the discipline of OD reach its current position of respectability

◆ Organizational Development has evolved along four main streams that are: Laboratory Training, Action Research, and Survey Feedback, Normative Approach, and the Productivity and Quality-of-work-life streams

◆ There are a number of models of planned change adopted by practitioners. Some popular ones are:

- Action Research model

- Lewin's three-step model

- Kotter's eight-step model

- Critical Research model

- Positive model / Appreciative Inquiry model

- Burke-Litwin model of organizational change

◆ A General model of planned change has been developed that takes in the best of all preceding models and becomes a uniform implementation model for practitioners to adopt.

Chapter **4**

Entry

This chapter is the first in a sequence of chapters that deal with the different stages of an OD intervention through the general model of planned change. This chapter provides an introduction to the process of 'entry' into an OD intervention which is the first stage.

Key learning objectives include the reader's understanding of the following:

- Introduction to the process of 'entry' into an OD intervention

- Why it is important to create a baseline against which future success can be achieved and measured.

- The responsibility of the leaders in the organization in the decision to initiate an intervention

- The tools they can call upon for support in that decision.

- The various types of OD practitioners that could be working on interventions.

- What a good OD proposal should consist of.

4.1 Initiating the Process of Planned Change

Like everything else in an organization, the process of initiation of change is also a decision that needs to be arrived at.

As mentioned earlier in the book, an organization is a deliberate animal, created for the purpose of striving for certain defined goals. It does not do anything because of its feelings or emotions, though it is possible that the feelings and emotions of people who take decisions on behalf of an organization sometimes guide their decisions.

How, then, does such an organization enter into an OD intervention? Or, how does it engage in a dialog and agreement with an OD practitioner for the purpose of implementing change? How does it initiate the process of planned change? How does it even know what to change?

The work of an organization gets carried out through its human agents. There are people who are assigned the responsibility of ensuring that the organization is able to achieve, or at least move towards its goals. There is a management structure or organizational structure that is implemented that defines the roles of the people involved. These roles, again, are defined with the objective of success for the organization.

The people involved could have different functional responsibilities, such as Human Resources for some and Finance for others. The people could have different quantities of responsibilities, such as sales in an area for an Area Sales Manager and the well-being of the entire organization for the CEO. An organization could also have many different groups and teams created with the sole objective of smoothening its march towards the defined goals.

Leaders expected to identify need

There is no single or definite formula for initiating an OD intervention. This is usually left to the discretion of the leaders who, by virtue of their position and role, are expected to have an understanding of what is going right and what is not. If they are good enough to lead the organization, they should be good enough to have an understanding of the need for improvement. A departmental head is expected to be able to take the view for the departments he/she heads while the CEO is expected to be able to take the decision for the entire organization. This is not to say that they do not have anyone to consult for this important decision. All the usual decision-making channels are in place. However, as being the most impacted parties on account of derailment of the company or a part of it, they are expected to be the most vigilant when it comes to the need for change.[11]

There are, of course, many tools and support systems they can rely on.

- Leaders keep track of the organization's performance. One of the key parameters for tracking is performance against expectation or against the goals defined. If the full-year revenue target is $100 million, and the first quarter has only yielded a revenue of $10 million against a target of $20

---

11. P. Block, "Flawless Consulting: A Guide to Getting Your Expertise Used," 3rd ed. (San Francisco: Jossey-Bass, 2011); C. Margerison, "Consulting Activities in Organizational Change," Journal of Organizational Change Management 1 (1988): 60–67; R. Harrison, "Choosing the Depth of Organizational Intervention," Journal of Applied Behavioral Science 6 (1970): 182–202.

million for the first quarter, the full-year target could be in jeopardy and would require attention.

- Keeping track of competitors could also yield important clues. If competitors are employing 100 people for realizing every million dollars of revenue while your company is employing 150 people for the same, maybe they know something that you don't. This could call for an overhaul of the present system.

- Any significant event taking place in the life of an organization, such as a merger or acquisition that is likely to cause uncertainty and turmoil could be a case for an OD intervention or a set of them.

- Customer feedback and surveys could also provide important inputs that may lead to questioning existing beliefs and introducing new thoughts and processes and systems.

However, the examples defined above are supposed to provide food for thought and triggers for the leaders to pay attention to. There could be valid reasons for the performance being the way it is, without requiring additional attention.

Moreover, the initiation does not have to start with a problem. It could even be for the purpose of leveraging an opportunity that might exist.

We need to remember that triggering an OD intervention is also a cost for the organization as it consumes resources and attention. As with everything else, the value it delivers needs to be ascertained to the extent possible before it is introduced.

The identification of an organization's need for change is the point of 'entry' for an OD intervention to ensue.

4.2 OD Practitioners

The OD practitioner/s tasked with the responsibility for the change can come from different sources:

Team members wear an OD hat

Some organizations follow a decentralized approach to the process. Many of the employees are provided training and expected to take on additional responsibility for identification as well as execution of OD interventions. Depending on the nature of the requirement, team members could be drawn from various functions and departments. This type of structure tends to be more informal than a structure with an OD specialist in the mix.

Internal OD team

Many large organizations have so much change going on all the time, in different locations, functions, and verticals that they find it worthwhile to invest in a team of OD experts who are on the rolls of the organizations and available to jump in any time there is a need. This is a more formal arrangement than the previous one, with the OD practitioner expected to ensure that the team follows the discipline set forth for such tasks. The OD practitioner, being an in-house expert, may not have a choice in terms of the interventions he/she is required to support.

External OD practitioners

As the name suggests, it is a variation of the internal OD team structure where the expert is an external consultant. As is to be expected, this would perhaps be carried out with the most formality, with the external expert being expected to add value based on his/her expertise in the subject. However, as it is an engagement between two independent parties, they can both exercise choice; the practitioner in terms of which initiatives to get involved with and the organization in terms of which practitioners to engage for the assignment.

4.3 Developing the OD Proposal

The 'entry' phase is expected to result in the definition of the objectives of initiating an OD intervention; what problem is sought to be solved or what opportunity is sought to be encashed. This helps in reaching a common baseline in order that the people and teams involved in the process have a common understanding and are able to work harmoniously together for the good of the organization. Without a common baseline, people could end up pulling in different directions based on their own understanding and vision. This phase, by outlining the issues and goals, serves to also set parameters for subsequent phases.

The first step would be for the organization or team interested in launching an intervention to articulate the problems or objectives. It is expected that all material information will be made a part of this articulation. If they have an inkling of the reasons for the problem or the means to the higher plane of performance, they should articulate that as well, even though it might only be a hunch based on the symptom at this stage. Subsequent steps will be carried out in more specific terms.

This step also involves collecting data and creating a baseline measurement of parameters. If the objective is to take revenues to $40 million per quarter, the fact that it is not $40 million today, but $10 million, needs to be recorded and acknowledged by all participants, so that subsequent disagreement does not erupt regarding the scale of change. However, at this stage, the data collection is limited to some key parameters. Subsequent stages may require a lot more data collection and analysis. In some cases, it is also possible that discoveries and learnings of subsequent phases may lead to a review and restatement of the goals of the intervention.[12]

The deliberations of this phase result in an output that is called the OD Proposal or the OD Contract (typically where the OD practitioner is an external party). It defines the reasons for initiating the intervention, expectations from it (or success criteria), parties that will be involved, the roles they will play, the resources expected to be consumed, and the broad rules or terms of reference, under which it will operate. It can also be called a Project Charter. The clearer and more specific it is, the greater the chance of cohesion in the team and the greater their chance of success.

---

12. D. Jamieson, "Pre-Launch," in Practicing Organization Development, 2nd ed., ed. W. Rothwell and R. Sullivan (San Francisco: Pfeiffer, 2005); J. Fordyce and R. Weil, Managing WITH People, 2nd ed. (Reading, MA: Addison-Wesley, 1979).

4.4 A Sample OD Proposal

A Sample OD Proposal prepared by a bank

Background information

Customer Satisfaction scores delivered by us are a key measure of performance delivered by our representatives. Delivering CSAT scores meeting and exceeding threshold levels set by clients will enable us to protect business volumes and gain wallet share.

Problem statement

Our CSAT scores are 4% below the client threshold level of 75% and could result in us losing business.

(Note: The more sharply a problem statement is defined, the greater the chances of cohesive effort at solving it. The problem statement that says "We think our CSAT scores are not as good as they can be" would not provide a starting point that is defined well enough.)

Goal Statement

Increase the CSAT scores to 75%.

(Note: This emanates almost directly from the problem statement, and specifies the end state and the point at which the OD intervention has been successful in delivering the desired result when the articulated problem has been resolved. There is usually a time factor included in the goal statement. It cannot be an indeterminate or indefinite effort. Hence, the goal statement might look like "Increase the CSAT scores to 75% within 90 days.")

Scope (Boundaries)

The following performance parameters should not be worse than their present levels which are defined as:

Handling time: 70 seconds per transaction

Agent cost: $20 per hour

(Note: This ensures that in trying to improve one parameter, the other parameters do not slip. It might be easy to increase the time spent with a customer to handle an issue. It might also be easy to start hiring resources who are more qualified, and perhaps more expensive, who could deliver a better experience. However, both these actions could jeopardize the business model. Hence, specifying boundaries ensures that the other parameters do not suffer. What is in scope and what is not could also be defined.)

Resources and roles

OD practitioner – the expert

Sponsor – the responsible manager/leader who will authorize budgets and resource allocation

Team members – roles to be defined

Timeline

Entry – 1st January

Diagnosis – 1st February

Implementation (Action Plan) – 1st March

Evaluation – 1st April

Institutionalization – 1st May

Quiz

1. In an organization, planned change is initiated by:

    a. Only the CEO

    b. Any one of the departmental heads

    c. Any one of the functional heads

    d. Any of the above

2. The financial MIS of the organization is a source based on which an OD intervention could be contemplated.

    a. Agree

    b. Disagree

3. When can an OD intervention be initiated?

    a. Only when the organization is facing a problem

    b. Only when there is an opportunity that can be leveraged

    c. Neither **a** nor **b**

    d. Either **a** or **b**

4. **Which of the following might not be the reason for entering into an OD intervention?**

   a. Announcement of a new product launch by a competitor

   b. Internal announcement of the organization shutting down a product line

   c. Customer survey indicating falling ratings

   d. An acquisition of a smaller competitor

5. **An OD intervention can be initiated even if there is no problem identified.**

   a. Agree

   b. Disagree

6. **Which of the problem statements given here would be an example of a well-defined problem statement?**

   a. We think our CSAT scores are not as good as they can be.

   b. Our CSAT scores are 4% below the threshold level of 75% and could result in us losing business.

   c. We need to push our CSAT scores to the highest possible level

   d. Our major competitor has grown revenues faster than we have in the last quarter

7. **Please select the most appropriate goal statement for an OD intervention.**

   a. We need to increase the CSAT scores to 75% plus

   b. Our CSAT score should be the best in the industry

   c. The CSAT score should show an upward trajectory

   d. None of the above

8. **Defining the scope helps in: (select all applicable)**

   a. Improving the company's profitability

   b. Reducing wastage of time on unrequited activities

   c. Ensuring other parameters do not deteriorate while improving one parameter

   d. Reducing infighting in the company

9. **The cost that will be incurred on an OD intervention is irrelevant once a senior leader has decided to 'enter' into one.**

   a. True

   b. False

10. The phase that follows the 'Enter' phase is known as

   a. Institutionalize

   b. Evaluate

   c. Monitor

   d. Diagnose

Answers	1 – d	2 – a	3 – d	4 – b	5 – a
	6 – b	7 – a	8 – b, c	9 – b	10 – d

Chapter Summary

◆ There is no single or definite formula for initiating an OD intervention. Leaders at the organization or department level, are expected to be engaged adequately with the business to identify the need for change.

◆ A problem need not be the only reason for an OD intervention. A perceived opportunity could also be a valid reason for one.

◆ Many different sources can provide information based on which 'entering' into an OD intervention may be considered appropriate, such as internal MIS, competitor initiatives, and customer feedback.

◆ An OD practitioner need not only be an external expert. It could also be an internal resource of the organization, or even team members trained to play the role.

◆ An OD proposal is developed as the exit from the 'entry' phase. It defines the status quo and captures the goals expected to be delivered by the OD intervention.

◆ A sample OD Proposal has been created that can serve as a template for others that may need to be created.

Chapter 5

Diagnosis

This chapter introduces the process of diagnosis and compares the organizational diagnosis process with medical diagnosis, which is a commonly understood process, to illustrate.

Key learning objectives include the reader's understanding of the following:

- The starting point of the process of diagnosis

- Techniques for identifying the starting point/s.

- The value of objectivity and transparency in organizations.

- Data collection techniques

- Techniques for narrowing down the variables on which data should be collected

- Commonly used statistical techniques for analysis of data

5.1 The Process of Diagnosis

Once a need has been identified, the natural next step is to find out, or investigate the reasons why it is the way it is. This phase provides an understanding of the challenges and barriers that might lie in the path to improvement. Have any attempts been made in the past to address the issue? If yes, what was the outcome?

Diagnosis consists of the steps, or series of steps, that establish the present status quo of the organization specific to the areas where improvement is sought. Understanding the status quo also involves developing an understanding of its drivers. Some of the types of questions that might need answers are:

- Why is the revenue in the quarter $10 million and not a different number?

- What are the variables that can impact this number, either positively or negatively?

- Are there some low-hanging fruits that could be plucked without much effort?

This is not to say that diagnosis does not take place in an organization if there is no OD intervention planned. Quite the contrary, the process of diagnosis and implementation keeps happening all the time as the people involved in a process seek fixes for issues they see as plaguing their area of responsibility. An OD intervention is a kind of acceptance that the day-to-day process of diagnosis and cure has not had the desired results and now needs to be moved to a higher plane of action that stands a better chance of making a difference via a designated, empowered set of people.

Comparison with medical diagnosis

The process of diagnosis is often associated by us with medical practice. If you are suffering from an ailment, a medical doctor will attempt to diagnose the underlying causes of the ailment and attempt to prescribe a cure for it. Oftentimes, multiple rounds of diagnosis and prescription have to be undergone as one possibility is eliminated and the intervention moves on to the other likely possibilities.

The process of diagnosis in OD is similar in some ways and different in other ways from a medical diagnosis.

How is it similar?

Like in medical practice, a patient (the organization) seeks help from an expert (OD practitioner) for a problem being experienced. The expert draws upon the skills and experience gained through working with the same or similar problems with other patients and drawing up a possible list of solutions which is then whittled down after more investigation or through trial and error.

How is it different?

In medical practice, a patient having a problem is real. It is never the case that the patient has sought medical help because the problem may not be there. In the case of an organization, however, it is possible that what is being perceived as a problem may not be a problem at all. However, that can only be established after it has been looked into. Delivering $10 million revenue against a target of $20 million is perceived as a problem. However, it is possible that there was an industry-wide issue and that competitors have only been able to achieve less than 50% of their target sales, and that the unused demand will come back in the next quarter.

The patient (organization) is a part of the process of finding a solution, guided by the steadying hand of the expert. In case of a medical condition, the patient expresses the problem but it is mostly left to the expert to explore and find solutions.

Also, while a medical expert's help is sought only in case of a problem, an OD expert's help may be sought not only for addressing a perceived problem but also for developmental goals, encashing an opportunity, or making the organization stronger to take on future challenges with gusto.

5.2 Diagnosis of Organizational Systems

When viewed as open systems, organizations can be diagnosed at three levels – organizational, group, and individual.

The open-systems model recognizes that an organization is a unit within the larger environment, which comprises everything that is external to the organization. The environment influences the working of the organization and is, in turn, influenced by it. Being a unit within the environment, the organization must act in consonance with the laws the environment has established, take inputs from it, process and transform them and return them to the environment in the form of finished goods and services. The outcome of this 'giving back' is the feedback an organization receives about its effectiveness.

The Table 5.1 below represents an established model for the diagnosis of open systems at these three levels. At each level, there are:

1. Inputs that the system has to work with

2. Key components for designing the system to create; in other words, the tools available for transforming the input

3. The system's outputs

Table 5.1   **Models of analysis of open systems**

	Organization	Group	Individual
Input	• General, task as well as created environment	• Design and culture of the organization	• Design and culture of the organization • Group setup and personal traits
Variables	• Strategy • Technology • HR systems • Management systems • Culture	• Group composition • Task structure • Goal clarity • Team alignment • Group norms	• Task identity and significance • Skills • Autonomy • Performance feedback
Output	• Organizational effectiveness	• Team effectiveness	• Individual's effectiveness

It is to be understood that each level is impacted by the functioning of the higher level. As an example, organizational design and culture are inputs for both the Group as well as the Individual levels.

As also discussed earlier, one of the keys to unlocking the issue is knowing what to look for. While the challenge may be known, what is causing the challenge is not known. At best, there are some thoughts and ideas, even guesses, about possible reasons. Getting to the relevant variables speedily is relevant across all three levels. This facilitates and energizes the diagnosis process.

5.3 Identifying Relevant Variables

Questions that OD practitioners often face are 'Where to start?" or "What to look for?"

In a world of information symmetry, a huge amount of information is available or can be collected. The challenge now is to ensure that we are looking for the right information.

While in many cases, the starting point could be obvious, there are also techniques that are used to arrive at a short list of variables that may be more relevant than others. Many of these techniques center around the concept of brainstorming - a free-flowing and unhindered flow of ideas and options with the potential of throwing up clues. These techniques try to synthesize the effort in order to ensure that they do not veer off the track and are able to create ideas with limited time and resources available.

One such technique is the 'Fishbone analysis,' or 'Ishikawa diagram,' after the founder of the technique.[13]

---

13. Kaoru Ishikawa, "Introduction to Quality Control," Productivity Press

| Figure 5.1 | Illustration of the Fishbone Analysis technique |

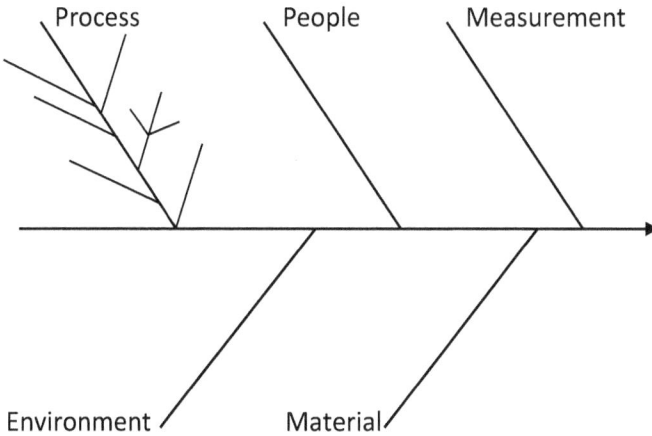

Fishbone analysis is a Graphic tool that displays possible causes of the problem. The purpose is to identify the possible causes of the problem or outcome.

Shown here is one system used by practitioners for breaking up the causes.

If a restaurant is trying to do a Fishbone Analysis to zero in on reasons for falling sales, it might classify poor quality of packing material and incorrect size of pans under Material and inadequate training and poor service under People. They might want to dig deeper into the training aspect and further break it down into inadequate time for training, incorrect hires, and no practical experience. These become areas they can choose from to address, depending on their evaluation of impact.

Each possible cause could be further broken down to a lower level, hence more branches, or bones, could be added to the figure of the fish. In order to lick off the brainstorming, certain headers that seem suitable to the leaders could be affixed, as in the diagram above.

At each step, asking the question "Why does this happen?" could result in a lower-level cause. The causes identified are clustered along logical areas to be looked into more deeply. There could also be a view taken to disregard some that may be considered to be less important or relevant and focus attention on a few items.

5.4 Data Collection

The diagnosis phase usually involves the collection of data to establish the status quo as well as for hints or clues the data might throw up that would lead to the identification of variables that could enable us to achieve our goals.

Data can be collected unobtrusively or obtrusively.

Unobtrusive data collection

People who are not working on the initiative do not come to know that an exercise of data collection is underway. Hence, this is perhaps the method that yields the most natural and accurate data as the identified goals for the intervention have probably been drawn on the basis of similarly collected data. Moreover, it provides data in the form of a time series that enables drawing conclusions in terms of the trajectory.

The common sources of such data are organizational records such as MIS and reports that are published on various subjects.

They could be profitability related or they could be staff attrition related. They could be production-related or they could be related to successful bids made by the organization.

This method, though free of human bias, could suffer from its own systemic bias. If a process change alters the trajectory of the data being collected, this method, being purely focused on the data, might not be able to correctly ascribe reasons for the change in trajectory.

Obtrusive methods of data collection

Obtrusive methods of data collection rely on the involvement of people for data to be collected. The people involved could be the data collectors, people engaged in the OD intervention, or even people who are unrelated to it.

The common methods are detailed below:

Observations

The data collector gets involved in the process, and independently observes and notes the aspects of the work on which data needs to be collected. The data collector could, for instance, stand at the point of entry to the workplace and note the number of people coming in after their scheduled time.

The data so collected, unless grouped together in some manner in order to identify leading trends may end up being textual observations that may not lend themselves to much analysis. Otherwise, as an independent, impartial observer, the data collector could collect valuable data.

Interviews

Interviews could be conducted individually or in groups. They could be structured or unstructured. Structured interviews will lend themselves more easily to data analysis as compared to unstructured ones that may require a lot of reading to make sense; and different sense to different people.

Interviews, especially when conducted individually, take a lot of time, which translates to cost. There is a self-report bias inherent in this method as the respondent will provide an answer that might be more acceptable rather than the real one. However, interviews continue to be a popular method of data collection.

Surveys

Surveys could be looked upon as structured, impersonal interviews. Each respondent provides responses to the same set of questions. If the responses are codified, the survey will lend itself to analysis. If the responses are textual, they will require a lot of effort to interpret.

5.5 Data Analysis – Quantitative Techniques

So far in this chapter, the focus has been on the collection of data that could lead the team to desired goals. However, data collection is not an end in itself. It is required only for the purpose of lending itself to analysis and drawing conclusions.

Hence, the next step after the collection of data is the analysis of data. Analysis may also influence the way data is collected as well as the pieces of information that are collected.

Central tendency

When we come across many numbers in a particular context, in order to derive meaning from them we need to convert them to a representative value. In other words, what is that one number which could represent the entire set? This becomes the representative 'central tendency' of that data set and is also known as summing up or summarizing the data.

The problem with data sets, especially with larger data sets, is that they are difficult to analyze. Consider the example given here.

| Table 5.2 | Marks obtained by 12 students in 2 subjects |

	A	B	C	D	E	F	G	H	I	J	K	L
History	20	20	30	20	50	80	60	60	60	60	10	40
Geography	60	20	30	40	40	40	40	50	50	60	50	50

This table represents the marks 12 students received in 2 subjects.

Just by looking at this data without any statistical tools, what would you say about the data?

- Would you say that students performed better in History or Geography?

- Which student do you think performed the best?

The most obvious way to do it is to calculate the central tendency of the data sets.

Mean

Mean, or arithmetic mean, is defined as the total sum of all data entries divided by the number of entries. Let us calculate the mean Customer Satisfaction Score for both processes. For this data set, at the subject level, the mean is:

Table 5.3 Calculation of mean per subject for the marks obtained

	A	B	C	D	E	F	G	H	I	J	K	L	Mean
History	20	20	30	20	50	80	60	60	60	60	10	40	42.5
Geography	60	20	30	40	40	40	40	50	50	60	50	50	44.2

We find that students have performed better in Geography compared to History.

Median

For the same data set, we now analyze the same problem from a different perspective; that of its median value. The Median is simply the 50th Percentile of a data set. In other words, it is the middle data point when all data points are arranged in ascending or descending order. If there are an even number of data points then we will have 2 middle points. In such a case the median is simply the mean of the two middle entries.

Reordering History in ascending order, we get:

Table 5.4 History marks reordered in ascending order

	K	A	B	D	C	L	E	J	G	H	I	F
History	10	20	20	20	30	40	50	60	60	60	60	80

The median is the mean of the middle values, L and E, 40 and 50, which is 45.

Reordering History in ascending order, we get:

Table 5.5	Geography marks reordered in ascending order

	B	C	D	E	F	G	H	I	K	L	A	J
Geography	20	30	40	40	40	40	50	50	50	50	60	60

The median is the mean of the middle values, G and H, 40 and 50, which is also 45.

The Median for process A is the mean of the 6th and 7th entries, i.e. 40 and 50= 45

The Median for process B is the mean of the 5th and 6th entries, i.e. 40 and 50= 45

Hence, what we see is that for the two subjects, two different measures of central tendency throw up different results. Thus, the purpose for which the tool is being used is a relevant and important consideration while calculating central tendency.

Mode

Yet another measure of central tendency is Mode.

Consider the previous example again, however, this time we will analyze it from a different perspective. We will attempt to find out the most likely score for the next transaction that will be performed.

This is known as the modal value or mode. It is the Most Frequently Occurring Value in a Data Set.

For History, the mode is 60, the most frequently occurring value. That means the next student in History has the highest chance of obtaining 60 marks.

For Process B the mode is 45 (40 and 50 occur 4 times each so we take the mean of the two). This means that a random student or the next student has the highest probability of obtaining marks between 40 and 50.

Note: The fact that this intermediate level is not defined is not relevant. In real life when we have huge datasets, we normally treat data to be continuous, meaning that every possible statistical value is present in the data set. In other words, it is possible to have each value in that distribution. As opposed to discrete data (as in this case) which is a defined, limited set of data points.

How do we decide which method to choose? That depends on what we are looking for. The following table summarizes the application:

Table 5.6	Application of measures of central tendency

Measure	Where to apply	Examples
Mean	• When we are concerned with average or general values.	• To find a general customer satisfaction score. • To find the average salary for employees.
Median/Percentile	• When we want to rank data points in a data set against each other.	• To find out the best/ worst performing employee. • To determine the most difficult to please customers.
Mode	When we are concerned with the likelihood of occurrence of an event or the value of a randomly picked instance.	• To find out how many days an employee is absent. • To find out how many customers are happy with the service they receive.

Standard Deviation and Variance

Consider the three data sets A, B, and C given below:

Table 5.7   **Three data sets**

A	B	C
5	2	−10
5	3	−5
5	4	0
5	5	5
5	6	10
5	7	15
5	8	20

Activity: Calculate the mean, median, and mode for A, B, and C.

You will find that they all have the same mean 5, the same median, which is 5, and the same mode, again 5. However, the three data sets are clearly different from each other.

In simple everyday terms, we might describe the third data set to be more 'spread out' as it ranges from −10 to 20, whilst the second data set ranges from 2 to 8 and is hence more 'together'. The first data set is completely 'together' as all values in it are 5. We need a way to quantitatively differentiate between such data sets, and that is where standard deviation comes in.

Standard deviation measures the deviation of a data set from its mean by finding the square root of the average of the square of the difference between each element and the mean. A data set with more 'spread out' distribution, such as C will have a high value of standard deviation whilst one with no spread, such as A, will have a standard deviation of 0.

Table 5.8	Three data sets with calculation of square of difference from mean

			Square of difference from Mean		
A	B	C	A	B	C
5	2	−10	0	9	225
5	3	−5	0	4	100
5	4	0	0	1	25
5	5	5	0	0	0
5	6	10	0	1	25
5	7	15	0	4	100
5	8	20	0	9	225
Variance (Average)			0	4	100
Standard deviation (Square root of average)			0	2	10

Note that the square of standard deviation gives us variance. If the entire formula is not put under the square root sign, we have the formula for variance. Variance is therefore simply the square of standard deviation. Theoretically, it means almost the same thing as standard deviation, however, it is rarely used as a statistical measure. We normally use standard deviation. This is because standard deviation, through first squaring and then square rooting, reverts back to the same scale as the original data set.

Correlation

Correlation is the statistical study of relationships between sets of data. It is positive if both quantities increase or decrease simultaneously (as in the case of ice cream sales and temp) or negative if an increase in one quantity corresponds to a decrease in the other (as in the example of bird flu and chicken consumption).

Correlation analyses the level of dependence of one on the other. It is expressed in terms of a single number known as the coefficient of correlation which takes a value between –1 and 1. The most commonly used method is known as the Karl Pearson coefficient.

A coefficient of 1 means a perfect positive correlation. This means that as one quantity increases the other increases proportionally. As the coefficient moves away from 1 it means non perfect positive correlation. This means that as one quantity increases the other will also increase but not in perfect proportion. The more the deviation from perfect proportionality, the greater the move away from a coefficient of 1. A negative correlation is when one series increases, the other series decreases. If the pace is matching, it becomes a perfect negative correlation, represented by a value of –1. As we move away from –1 towards 0, the correlation becomes more and more imperfect than negative correlation.

Scattergram

A scattergram is a visual representation of the relationship between two variables. It plots points on the graph that represent the values of the two variables for a particular event.

Figure 5.2 **Illustration of a positive Scattergram correlation**

Positive correlation

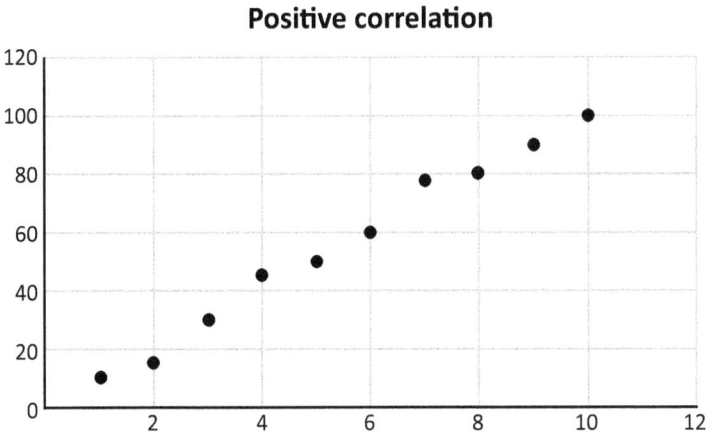

As the X-axis value increases, so does the Y-axis value. An example is the sale of ice cream with a rise in temperature during the summer months. As the temperature rises, so do sales of ice cream.

Figure 5.3 **Illustration of a negative Scattergram correlation**

Negative correlation

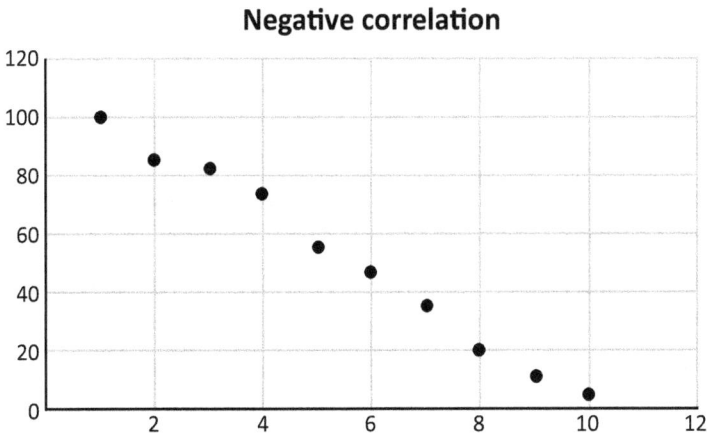

As the X-axis value increases, the Y-axis value decreases. An example is an ambient temperature mapped against the altitude when you go up a mountain. As the altitude increases, the temperature reduces.

Figure 5.4   **Illustration of a random Scattergram - no correlation**

No correlation

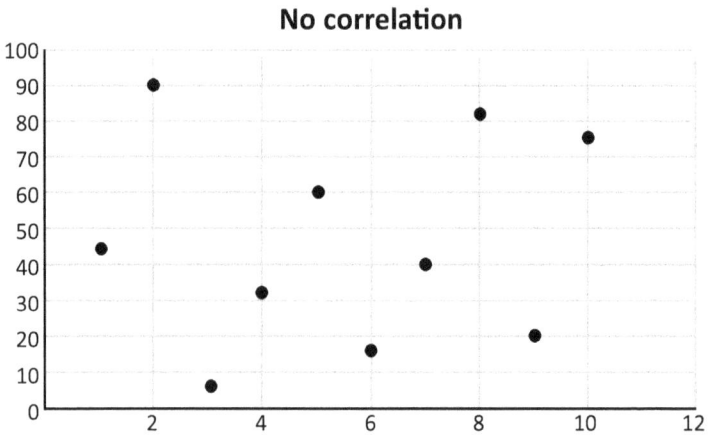

No defined relationship between the X-axis and Y-axis values

Pareto Analysis

Based on the Pareto Principle, that attributes 80% or more of the impact being the result of 20%, or less, of the attributable causes, Pareto Analysis is a powerful decision-support tool in the analysis of data. It is also known as the 80:20 rule and it applies to business as much as it does to life. 80:20 is a commonly used point of reference. The distribution could be different, such as 90:10 or 70:30.

While OD practitioners may be keen to change the world, they are constrained by real-world limitations of budgets, time, and resources. The Pareto Analysis enables them to identify and focus on the few areas that will result in a big impact on the outcome.

As an example, an organization is best with problems of poor satisfaction scores that are attributable to the following reasons:

Table 5.9 **Reasons for poor customer satisfaction scores**

Reason	Low score %
Rudeness of service agent	35
Inadequate knowledge	6
Customer wait time	25
Knowledge tool not updated	5
Incorrect call transfer	9
Inability to understand	20

If we do a Pareto Analysis, we will be able to identify the few reasons which, if addressed, would lead to removing 80% of the cause for dissatisfaction:

Figure 5.5	Dissatisfaction scores arranged on a Pareto Chart

Pareto Analysis

Reasons for low CSAT scores

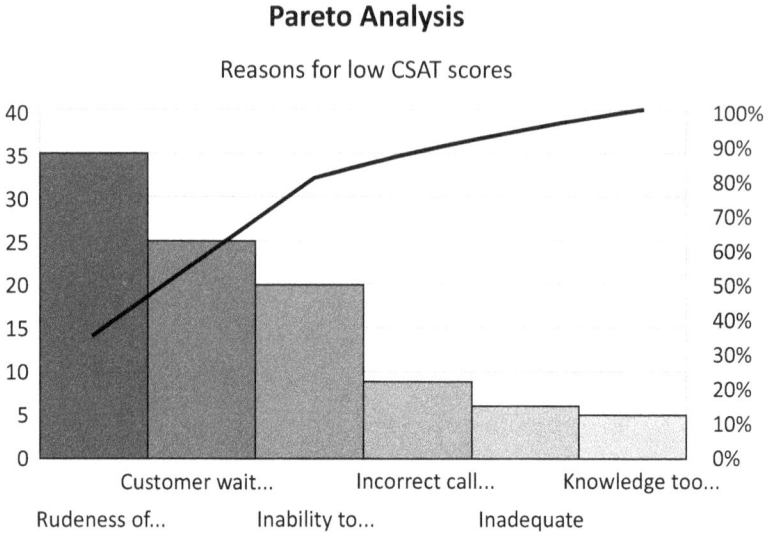

Control Impact Matrix

This is another prioritization tool that can be used when data is non-numeric.

There could be a variety of factors identified resulting in variance. The Control Impact matrix helps us in zeroing in on a few that should be prioritized.

Factors identified will be placed in one of the six boxes of the table, based on their expected level of impact on the problem and our ability to influence the factor or our control over it.

The factors falling in the top left box of the table below, which have a high level of impact and can be influenced by us, will become the natural first choice for implementation.

Figure 5.6 | **Illustration of Control Impact Matrix**

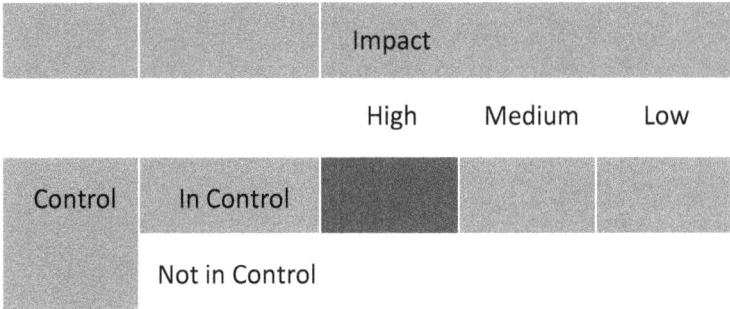

		Impact		
		High	Medium	Low
Control	In Control			
	Not in Control			

5.6 Data Analysis – Qualitative Techniques

Though quantitative data and analysis are preferred for the sense of objectivity it conveys, techniques for analysis of qualitative data have also been developed that facilitate the process and yield actionable output. In many cases, there may be no choice except to use qualitative analysis techniques as the underlying data is such. The two commonly used techniques are described here.

Content Analysis

Often, the data collected is in the form of text, or notes, that do not lend itself to any statistical analysis technique. Content analysis makes that possible.

A perusal of the text to get a broad understanding of the themes is needed. In most cases, a few prominent themes emerge from the text. Once the peruser has an understanding of the broad nature, he/she will attempt to create categories that best represent the themes that have been gleaned from the comments. Once that has been done, an attempt will be made to classify the comments into one of the themes that have been created.

Thus, in a way, it converts textual information to numeric data that can then be analyzed using one of the many quantitative analysis techniques available, if warranted. It must be understood, however, that for best results, the process of perusal and classification may need to be done by an expert in the field.

Force-Field Analysis

The force-field analysis method identifies two types of forces operating in the organization :[14]

- Forces for change

- Forces for maintaining the status quo or resisting change

Information on these forces is usually collected through obtrusive measures like interviews, observations, and questionnaires. The final output is to reach a rating or ranking of both types of forces in terms of their impact, or strength.

This process might need to be carried out in two steps:

1. Identifying the major forces of each type with the help of discussions and interviews.

2. Inviting people connected with the process to submit their observations/ratings/opinions on the list of forces so developed.

---

14. K. Lewin, Field Theory in Social Science (New York: Harper & Row, 1951)

Once the identification and assessment of the impact have been done, strategies need to be created to reduce the strength of the forces that are opposing change and strengthen the hand of the forces that are promoting change. According to Lewin, working on the forces that resist change is a better strategy for taking the organization to a higher plane of performance, as it produces a lower level of anxiety and tension in the organization.

Quiz

1. In the open-systems model, which of the following statements are true? (you can select more than one)

    a. Organization design is an input for group level diagnosis

    b. Group design is an input for organizational level diagnosis

    c. Individual design is an input for group level diagnosis

    d. None of the above

2. While a medical expert's help is sought only in case of a problem, an OD expert's help may be sought not only for addressing a perceived problem but also for developmental goals or encashing an opportunity.

    a. True

    b. False

3. In the open-systems model, diagnosis can be carried out at which of the following levels? (you can select more than one)

    a. Individual

    b. Group

    c. Organization

    d. Environment

4. **Which of the following are examples of obtrusive data collection?**

   a. Historical MIS

   b. Interviews

   c. Questionnaire-based surveys

   d. Shop Floor observations

5. **Collection of textual, or free format data tends to lend itself to analysis with greater difficulty than codified data. Which of the following data collection methods might provide textual data?**

   a. Historical MIS

   b. Interviews

   c. Questionnaire-based surveys

   d. Shop Floor observations

6. **If we plot ice cream sales and temperature on a scattergram, which of the following types of scattergrams are we likely to see?**

   a. No correlation

   b. Positive correlation

   c. Negative correlation

7. **If you were trying to answer the question, "how rapidly does chicken consumption decrease with the increase in the spread of bird flu", which statistical tool would you use?**

   a. Central tendency

   b. Standard deviation

   c. Pareto Analysis

   d. Correlation

8. **In a data series where more values are being added, if we were to estimate the likely value of the next entry to the database, which tool will we use?**

   a. Mean

   b. Median

   c. Mode

   d. Variance

9. **Which of the following might be the result of a Pareto Analysis? (you can select more than one)**

   a. 40% of employees do 60% of work

   b. 60% of employees do 40% of the work

   c. 30% of drivers cause 70% of accidents

   d. 20% of clothes in the wardrobe are worn 80% of the time

10. Which of the following techniques are useful for the analysis of qualitative data?

    a. Pareto Analysis

    b. Median

    c. Content Analysis

    d. Scatterplot

Answers	1 – a	2 – a	3 – a, b, c	4 – a, b, c	5 – b, d
	6 – b	7 – d	8 – c	9 – all correct	10 – c

Chapter Summary

◆ An organization operates like an open system, taking from the environment and giving back to it.

◆ Organizational diagnosis can be understood through a comparison with the process of medical diagnosis, though there are some differences between the two.

◆ One needs to identify the variables about which data is to be collected. Methods like the Fishbone Diagram aid the process of brainstorming for this identification.

◆ Data can be collected through Obtrusive or Unobtrusive methods. Obtrusive methods provide current information but are visible to the people about whom data is being collected and hence may not be natural responses.

◆ There are several commonly used methods of statistical analysis of collected data such as central tendency, variance, correlation, and Pareto Analysis that aid decision-making.

◆ Techniques like Content Analysis and Force-field analysis are available for analysis of textual or non-numeric data.

Chapter 6

Implementation (Action Plan)

This chapter provides an understanding of what an intervention is, while discussing the implementation of one.

Key learning objectives include the reader's understanding of the following:

- What is an intervention

- Types of interventions

- Areas addressed by different types of interventions

- The process of change

- Sequence of steps designed to ensure success for the intervention

6.1 Overview of Interventions

Having analyzed the data and reached some conclusions regarding the changes that would benefit the organization and drive it towards the stated goals, the OD process moves on to the stage of action planning and implementation.

The objective of the exercise being to create change, the next phase involves action planning, or creating a plan that would be able to take the organization towards its desired goal as envisioned when the process of change was initiated. This is the stage at which identification of resources is done, approvals obtained, and responsibilities portioned out amongst the team members driving the change. Equally important is the setting up of goals and parameters through which its achievement, or lack of it, could be measured.

For example, the Diagnosis phase might tell us that distance from the place of work has a bearing on people being absent frequently but it does not tell us what to do about it. The choice of what to do becomes an intervention. As always, there will be many possible interventions in a given situation that one might need to choose from, keeping in mind the goal as well as the principles of the OD discipline.

OD interventions usually involve setting in motion a series of planned activities designed to achieve the goals with which the intervention was conceptualized. Disturbing the status quo is to be expected; that, in fact, is the core purpose of the intervention. A need was felt for the change which should be delivered through an OD intervention.

6.2 Types of Interventions

They include four major types of planned change:

Human Process Interventions

These interventions focus on people within organizations and the processes of leadership, communication, problem solving, and decision making used for the accomplishment of organizational goals. These interventions are built upon the framework of human psychology and human relations, with fulfillment of people being a key driver to organizational effectiveness.

One of the most frequently applied sets of interventions include the ones related to interpersonal relationships and group dynamics. Through techniques like Process consultation, Third-party intervention, and Team building, OD consultants help group members diagnose group functioning issues and devise appropriate solutions to process problems with the goal of equipping group members with the skills to be able to do it themselves in the future.

Another set of human process interventions has a wider remit than individuals and groups and addresses the total organization or a significant part of it. Through interventions like Organization confrontation meetings, intergroup relations, and large-group interventions, these interventions get people to participate in the process of identifying problems and finding solutions. The composition of the group might vary depending on the problem at hand.

Technostructural Interventions

People have always been a critical resource in organizations that have made efforts to employ and harness them in a manner most likely to produce the best results for the organization. Technology has, over the last few decades, emerged as the great force multiplier. OD is paying more attention to these two elements in an effort to introduce planned change in organizations.

Based on engineering philosophies, in addition to psychology and sociology, a combination of productivity and human fulfillment is stressed.[15]

Interventions that work with the structure (or restructuring) of organizations:

Structural design – This change process addresses how work is divided and organized. It could involve moving from legacy structures to more modern processes and customer-based structures.

Downsizing – The effort here is to separate the required from the not required elements and then pare down the ones not required, including personnel layoffs.

Reengineering – Processes and workflow is the center of attention, with the effort focused on improving them so that either more can be done with the same or the same can be done with less. Usually, enabling technology forms the backbone of this change.

---

15. Review of Psychology 25 (1974): 313–41. 2. E. Lawler III, The Ultimate Advantage (San Francisco: Jossey-Bass, 1992); F. van Eijnatten, A.B. Shani, and M. Leary, "Socio-Technical Systems: Designing and Managing Sustainable Organizations," in Handbook of Organization Development, ed. T. Cummings (Thousand Oaks, CA: Sage Publications, 2008), 277–309

Interventions that involve employees in decision-making and strive to move the center of gravity toward the lower reaches of the hierarchy:

Parallel structures – Involves members in resolving ill-defined, complex problems and provides parallel structures, such as quality circles, that provide an alternative setting for seeking solutions.

Total quality management – The mantra of quality is spread across the organization, with the support of training for a wide cross-section. Members are expected to apply this knowledge in striving for continuous improvement in all spheres.

High-involvement organizations – This comprehensive intervention designs almost all features of the organization to promote high levels of employee involvement. A widely dispersed decision-making process is promoted through targeted changes.

Interventions involving engineering, motivational, and sociotechnical systems application to work design:

Job enrichment – Creates jobs that employees find fulfilling leading to improved job satisfaction and performance.

Self-managed work teams – This intervention designs work for teams performing highly interrelated tasks that require real-time decision-making. Self-managed work teams are typically responsible for a complete product or service and members are able to make decisions and control their own task behaviors without a lot of external controls

Human Resources Management Interventions

As organizations have gone global, their human resource imprint has also expanded, raising the profile of human resource management in the modern organization.

Besides, since many of the OD interventions have a human angle to them, there has always been an interest in looking at the two disciplines together. As opposed to the human process interventions covered earlier, this section addresses the management of the resources that are there.

There are a number of sub-disciplines that have emerged as a result, such as recruitment and selection, career management, skilling, goal-setting and performance management, employee wellness, and several others. The key belief is that people being key resources, managing them better will lift the performance of the organization.

Interventions concerning performance management

Setting goals – Well begun is half done, they say. Setting realistic as well as challenging goals sets the right expectations and a benchmark on which future performance discussions can be based.

Performance appraisal – This is the eventual outcome of goal setting. If there is no appraisal to be done, then there might not be any need for goals.

Feedback – While feedback is not expected to be dependent on performance appraisal and should be done throughout the performance period, the appraisal does create an opportunity for a robust discussion.

Rewards – This is what most employees work for and hence getting it right is of importance. The goal, as always, is to ensure that it results in the right behavior that moves the organization forward, and not empty the bank.

Interventions for developing and retaining talent

These types of interventions focus on the retention and development of talent so that they can contribute more.

Mentoring – Often deploys a one-on-one strategy for interaction between an OD practitioner and the client. It covers personal learning that is expected to translate to organizational benefits.

Leadership development – These interventions seek to build competencies that are relevant to the organization. The methods vary, such as classroom training, e-learning, simulations, case studies, etc. depending on the subject and the organizational comfort.

Career planning and development – The focus here is retention, with the understanding that an employee will contribute more as he/she matures. It strives to demonstrate a growth path for individuals, usually managerial staff.

Wholesome interventions – While these interventions may not address a specific organizational need, they are required in the modern world.

Managing workforce diversity – This seeks to create an open and accepting culture where difference is celebrated and seen as a resource that strengthens the organization.

Employee stress and wellness – In a world of stress and competition, the personal lives of employees cast a shadow on their performance at work. It is important for organizations to address these issues and enable employees to be supported in order that their full potential can be realized by the company.

Strategic Change Interventions

These interventions do not fit into one specific area and are usually organization-wide in scope. They draw from various disciplines and seek to bring an alignment between the various forces that pull the organization in multiple directions.

Design of organization – This could be looked upon as an 'umbrella' intervention. Large organizations have many moving parts that need to work with each other for the best results. This strategy seeks to rebalance this alignment.

Culture – Once again, this is a core element that exerts a significant influence on the outcomes. Many experts say that culture is an outcome and is not actionable. This strategy seeks to influence organizational culture and ensure that it is homogeneous so that people pull in the same direction.

Learning – This intervention tries to increase the organization's capability to open themselves up to external influences and continually acquire and develop new knowledge in a bid to stay relevant.

Self-correcting – This remains one of the final frontiers for OD practitioners. They want their interventions to result in an organization that is able to identify the need for change and make the transition, all on its own. Organizations learn how to design and implement their own strategic changes. These are adaptable organizations that are open to change.

Mergers and acquisitions – The focus here is on addressing key strategic, leadership, and cultural issues prior to a legal and financial transaction that leads to the merger of two organizations followed by subsequent operational integration.

Alliances – Seeking out like-minded organizations with the objective of making the sum of their gains greater than what they would be able to achieve individually drives this initiative. Operationalizing such an alliance involves working with people, intellectual property, technology, capital as well as physical infrastructure and assets.

Networks – While alliances is the term used when two organizations come together for reciprocal benefit, when more than two organizations come together it becomes a network.

6.3 Leading the Change

People, as well as organizations, prefer the safety of the status quo and not the uncertainty that change usually brings. For any change to be effective, it needs to be handled with kid gloves. OD experts generally advise a set of steps to be followed for implementation to be effective. These are to be followed sequentially, though they can, at times, also happen in parallel.

Creating motivation for change

Unless there are compelling reasons for it, why change? That is the position most individuals and organizations will take. Like they say, "if it ain't broke, why fix it?"

That might be the point OD interventions have to battle against in forward-looking organizations that make an effort to see the future and change themselves in time, in a planned way. Individuals and groups in the organization, who are not able to see that need are likely to resist. Of course, if the situation is so dire that there is really no choice, the job of motivating change becomes easy for OD practitioners. However, some would argue that that is not planned change, that is more like forced change.

In a mature world, in order to create readiness for change, OD specialists need to educate participants and create a virtual crystal ball for them so that they are able to understand what the future holds for them. It is a process of sensitization. It is helpful if they can call upon additional resources that convey the same message. It is to be expected that the organization's leaders will be on board and amplify these messages. Competitors performing better could be invoked to create a picture of the desired future.

There will be resistance, as well as the deniers. Overcoming this resistance is as important as creating the motivation for change. Each individual and group will react from his/her/their own perspective and past. Objections need to be handled with sensitivity and empathy. Open communication tends to build confidence rather than sidebars with groups who are objecting. Including representatives from different groups, not just the objecting ones, will also create confidence in the planning.

Creating a Vision

Naysayers deride the creation of vision as a fanciful exercise that has no connection with actual performance. Believers swear by it and offer data on organizations with a clear and challenging vision consistently outperforming their peers.[16]

While creating consensus on how the planned change will take the organization closer to the vision, sometimes the change can be so fundamental that it might require mulling over the vision statement itself, and it would still hold good. Many times, this process is undertaken through activities like offsite meetings that permit a free flow of thoughts.

Participation is encouraged as that is seen as a sign-up or commitment to the vision. Creation of the vision and getting subscriptions to it, in some ways, is similar to the need for creating a picture of the future. However, in this case, it is now a specific exercise and statement.

The process usually entails a shared discovery of the organization's ideology or vision, and constructing the future vision, if different, together.

Getting political support

Wherever there are people, there are likely to be interpersonal dynamics at play. Though the organizational vision is common, each individual and group within it has a different role to play. We already know that change threatens the status quo. It also threatens the balance of power between groups and individuals.

In some ways, these various steps are interconnected. Getting political support is like creating motivation and overcoming

---

16. Collins and Porras, Built to Last; T. Stewart, "A Refreshing Change: Vision Statements That Make Sense," Fortune, September 30, 1996, 195–96; T. Stewart, "Why Value Statements Don't Work," Fortune, June 10, 1996, 137–38

objections. However, the execution here is more targeted, as an attempt is first made to identify power centers and then address them through specific strategies.

A model now finding favor with OD practitioners was proposed by Greiner and Schein. [17]

They classified power into three sources and offered a strategy for addressing each.

| Table 6.1 | Sources of power and strategies for addressing | |

If the power source is	Power strategy to be used	Example
Knowledge	Play it straight	OD expert with subject knowledge
Personality	Use social networks	Charismatic individual who can inspire devotion
Others' support	Go around the formal system	Informal networks

In essence, one needs to assess the change agents and the source of power wielded by them, and then adopt a suitable strategy for bringing about the desired results.

---

17. Power and Organization Development: Mobilizing Power to Implement Change (Prentice Hall Organizational Development Series), 1st Ed. By Greiner, Larry E.; Schein, Virginia E., ISBN 0201121859. © 1988 Addison-Wesley Publishing Company Inc

Executing the Transition

This is the time for action and specifics.

From a shared vision developed earlier, the transition process now needs a micro-definition of tasks and events along with responsibilities and timelines for the pieces of the jigsaw to fit together. In present-day parlance, it is also referred to as 'project management.' Transitions are managed through the discipline of project management that not only keeps track of progress but also keeps adjusting the variables for optimum results while highlighting risks identified. Milestones are another feature of this phase. When the change is big, an 'all or nothing' approach can be disastrous. Hence, midway points, or milestones are defined. These serve to assure the change leaders that the transition is progressing along the right lines.

Special structures for managing the change process may need to be created as one would not like to jeopardize the functioning of the organization while the change is implemented. Equally, for the change to have focus, it should not become just one more responsibility of the managers. It is expected that this team will be staffed with people with the power to guide the change process through to its logical conclusion, and mobilize support when needed.

Often, sets of employees within the organization need to learn new skills to ensure that they are not left floundering in the dark when they reach the new organization. Hence, training is an important element of this stage.

Sustaining Momentum

If not careful, the organization might witness all changes being lost very quickly as the tendency to revert to old ways manifests itself, especially in stressful situations. Hence, sustained support needs to be provided to ensure that the change is embedded in the psyche and processes of the changed organization.

There are many new activities that are not required in normal circumstances, that will need to be done. Data collection, discussions, training, consultation, and workshops, all require resources. The organization needs to factor the time and expense and support it with a separate budget.

Attention should also be paid to the 'change agents' who are looked upon as the people who will be the catalysts for the change. While the rest of the staff may have each other to share experiences with, as leaders, in the forefront of an important transition, the change agents may not have such outlets. The organization should ensure that in the larger objective of attaining organizational level change, such groups are not left high and dry, as that could also impact the progress of the initiative. Creating a structure of 'shadow colleagues' is one ruse often used by OD practitioners for this group to bounce their thoughts and stresses off.

The relevance of rewards can never be underestimated. The organization needs to be ready with a reward and recognition program that rewards behavior that is desirable in the new organization.

Quiz

1. **Please select all statements that are true with regard to OD interventions:**

   a. An OD intervention is a set of sequenced and planned actions or events intended to help the organization increase its effectiveness.

   b. OD Interventions purposely disrupt the status quo.

   c. OD interventions need to be cleared by the CEO before being implemented.

   d. An OD intervention cannot be implemented without an OD expert.

2. **One of the requirements for the success of an OD intervention is that it should be based on the causal knowledge of intended outcomes.**

   a. True

   b. False

3. **Which of the following are interventions that are a part of human process interventions?**

   a. Alliances and Networks

   b. Culture Change

   c. Coaching

   d. Organization Confrontation Meeting

   e. Large-group Interventions

4. **Which of the following are interventions that are a part of techno-structural interventions?**

   a. Training and Development

   b. Third-party Interventions (Conflict Resolution)

   c. Intergroup Relationships

   d. Structural Design

   e. Reengineering

5. **Which of the following are interventions that are a part of human resource management interventions?**

   a. Process Consultation and Team Building

   b. Reward Systems

   c. Career Planning and Development

   d. Employee Stress and Wellness

   e. Mergers & Acquisitions

6. **Which of the following are interventions that are a part of strategic interventions?**

   a. Coaching

   b. Downsizing

   c. Career Planning and Development

   d. Integrated Strategic Change

   e. Self-designing Organizations

7. In the process of implementation of change, managing the transition through micro-level planning should be done before creating a vision for the future organization.

   a. True

   b. False

8. In the process of implementation of change, creating a motivation for change should be done before which of the following steps?

   a. Creating a shared vision of the future organization

   b. Developing political support that enables the overcoming of obstacles and provides impetus

   c. Managing the transition through micro-level planning and monitoring

   d. Sustaining momentum for all time to come

9. Select the activities relevant for overcoming resistance to change.

   a. Sensitize the organization to pressures for change

   b. Convey credible positive expectations for change

   c. Provide empathy and support

   d. Communicate

   e. Involve members in planning and decision making

10. If the source of the individual's power derives from Knowledge, the most suitable strategy for managing it would be:

    a. Asking for the individual's reassignment

    b. Playing it straight

    c. Using social networks

    d. Going around the formal system

Answers	1 – a, b	2 – a	3 – c, d, e	4 – d, e	5 – b, c, d
	6 – d, e	7 – b	8 – all correct	9 – c, d, e	10 – b

Chapter Summary

◆ An organizational development intervention is a sequence of activities, actions, and events intended to help an organization improve its performance and effectiveness as identified at the time of launch, in relation to the position at that time.

◆ Effective interventions are characterized by:

1. Relevance to the needs of the organization

2. Being based on causal knowledge of intended outcomes

3. Transference of competence to manage change to organization members

◆ OD interventions are classified into the following 4 types:

1. Human Process Interventions

2. Technostructural Interventions

3. Human Resources Management Interventions

4. Strategic Interventions

◆ The process of implementing change goes through the following sequence:

● Creating motivation for the change

● Creating a shared vision of the future organization

● Developing political support that enables the overcoming of obstacles and provides impetus

- Managing the transition through micro-level planning and monitoring

- Sustaining momentum for all time to come

Chapter 7

Evaluation

After plans have been implemented, it needs to be evaluated to see how successful they have been in driving towards the planned goals as that was the entire purpose of the exercise. This chapter will define Evaluation and describe the stages at which it should be done during the process of implementation of an OD intervention.

Key learning objectives include the reader's understanding of the following:

- The process of Evaluation after plans have been implemented

- The different types of Evaluation measures

- The stages at which Evaluation should be done during the process of implementation

- The role of variables in addition to the primary variable and connected to it

- The characteristics of good measures

- Suggestions for OD practitioners for overcoming some of the challenges inherent in measurement

7.1 What is Evaluation?

"An organization is a deliberate creature."

This phrase has probably been mentioned a number of times in this text to convey that all actions taken by an organization are thought-out acts, and not random ones. They are directed towards achieving the organizational goals, either directly, or indirectly through the achievement of stepping stones that will lead to the attainment of the larger goal.

If an action has been decided upon by the human brain that controls its actions, it is only logical that the organization also establish a mechanism to ascertain how successful or unsuccessful that action has been in achieving the goals for which it was launched. Even though it would be late for this particular action to be undone, the evaluation will, at least, help in providing learning that could be implemented in the future. Also, it helps in establishing responsibility.

If, for example, an organization decides to invest in training the staff of a particular section as it believes that that intervention would enhance engagement between the organization and the staff and reduce the rate at which they were resigning, which was a cause for great concern. The investment in training is real. If the organization has made that investment, it needs to know whether it has resulted in any improvement in the attrition issue that they were facing.

This process of evaluation is usually undertaken at two stages which will be covered in detail in the later parts of this chapter:

1. Implementation evaluation

2. Impact evaluation

In the context of OD interventions, research design, and measurement are two key parameters in the evaluation process.

7.2 Types of Evaluation of OD interventions

Implementation evaluation

Nothing can be taken for granted is one of the unwritten rules in life and in business. We do not have control over the future, though we believe we would like to. There are many unexpected events and variables that can derail our plans.

An implementation intervention is no different. It is launched with all good intentions, with the right plans and processes in place. Unlike a machine, where pressing the same button will produce the same response each time from all machines of the same kind, different humans will understand and process the same instruction differently. The organization can only specify the details up to a point. Beyond that, it is left to the sense and discretion of the individual receiving, interpreting, and executing it. There, naturally, some trial and error is involved.

An evaluation of the implementation process, thus, can enable the organization to head off such derailments at a reasonably early phase in the implementation cycle, saving significant rework if caught at a later stage.

Impact evaluation

Impact evaluation is a natural step in the process of implementation. Since an OD intervention has been determined to be the right course of action given a certain status quo, its implementation would be expected to produce a desired change in the organization.

How would one find out if the desired change has, indeed, been wrought? Through the process of an impact evaluation, also known as a post-implementation evaluation. Through an OD intervention, if an organization expects its attrition rate to reduce, it will only know if it performs an evaluation of the results after the implementation.

It is to be expected that the implementation process has been executed along expected lines, including the repetition of some cycles and steps resulting from discoveries during the implementation evaluation.

The evaluation methodology is typically specified before the intervention implementation has been initiated, as a part of the initiation phase. This ensures that the process is not abused by an interested party by being set up after the implementation is over and some understanding of the results has started emerging. It could be set up to show the results as being good or bad, depending upon the objectives of the so-called interested party evaluating the results.

7.3 Measurement

If an evaluation is to be done, either of implementation or of impact, it stands to reason that there is an evaluation measurement system that is in place.

It also stands to reason that the measurement system established for the evaluation of results is the same as, or similar to, the one that was used to identify the areas of improvement for addressing when the OD intervention was launched. Hence, the circle gets completed.

Measurement systems should not be created when evaluation needs to be done. They should be the product of the framework that is defined at the time an OD intervention is launched. The variables that denote the problem or challenge that needs to be fixed, should be the same variables used to measure the post-implementation impact. If employee absenteeism is the problem that is sought to be addressed, once the implementation is complete, measurement of employee attrition to evaluate the impact has no meaning. The measurement has to be based on achieving success on the initially identified variable and measured and calculated in the same manner.

Example

An organization measures employee attrition as follows:

(Employees at the beginning of month - employees no longer in the company at end of the month) / employees at beginning of the month)

Let us assume some numbers:

Employees at the beginning of the month = 1000

Employees no longer in the company at end of the month =80

(80 refers to employees who were a part of the 1000 at the start of the month but were not in the company at the end of the month. Hence, from the starting population, only 920 remained.)

The number of new employees who joined during the same period = 280.

Headcount at end of month = 1200

While the OD intervention was being designed and implemented, the organization, as part of a larger restructuring, changed the attrition calculation to:

[(Employees at the beginning of the month - employees no longer in the company at end of the month) / (employees at beginning of the month + employees at end of the month)2]

Using the original calculation, attrition would be:

(80/1000) = 8%

Using the new method, attrition would be:

[80/(1000+1200)/2]

= [80/1100] = 7.3%

Thus, the data yields different results and comparison with the status quo will be difficult. Therefore, one of the two approaches should be adopted:

1. Use the original formula to measure the success of the OD intervention

2. Go back and calculate the status quo using the new formula and then compare the post-implementation results. In some cases, it may not be possible to go back and calculate as some of the data points may not be available.

7.4 Other Things Remaining the Same

There is a concept known as the Iron Triangle used in Operations and Project management.

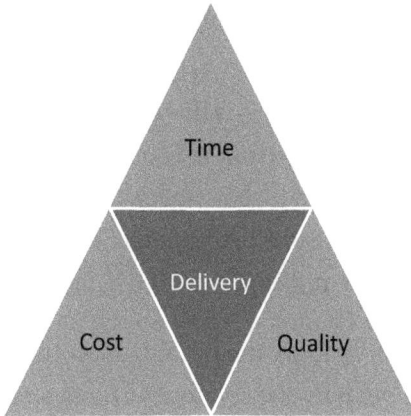

The three vertices of the Iron Triangle are:[18]

Quality – The quality of the output

Time – Time taken to produce the output

Cost – Resources consumed in producing the output

These three forces are understood to exert influence over the output and each organization operates in a certain equilibrium

---

18. What is the Iron Triangle of Project Management? (villanovau.com)

between the three. It is known as the Iron Triangle because the moment one of the three parameters is changed, it will impact at least one, if not both the other parameters:

- If we allow more time, it might result in better quality or lower cost

- If we reduce our quality expectation, it might enable us to do the work in lesser time or at a lower cost

- If we allocate more funds to it, we might be able to hire better resources and consequently deliver better quality or deliver the same in quicker time

How is this relevant?

When an OD intervention is initiated, there is a status quo that the organization is seeking to alter. The measured parameters may be few but there are a lot of underlying variables that exert an influence on that measured parameter. The organization is operating in a certain equilibrium between all those variables.

With an OD intervention, the organization seeks to bring about an improvement in one or more variables/parameters of measurement. It does not seek to bring about improvement in one variable at the cost of another.

As an example, if attrition is the target parameter, the organization could increase employee salaries which may reduce attrition. But that means an improvement in attrition at the expense of higher costs. While that may be the right strategy in some cases where it is assessed that the expense of the salary increase is far lower than the benefit to be gained by lower attrition, for the sake of illustration we will assume that that is not an option.

Hence, while measurement does need to take into account the target parameter being addressed by the OD intervention, it also needs to measure other variables that could impact or be impacted by it. The purpose of this is to ensure that the other parameters are not sliding downhill while improving the target parameter.

The only exception is where a slide in some cases has been accepted by the management as a better equilibrium for the sake of improvement in the target parameter.

7.5 Characteristics of good measures

Designing good measures form the bedrock of the evaluation process based on which the organization hopes to demonstrate improvement and change. What are the constituents of good measures?

The operational definition should be standardized and rigorous

A measure should mean the same thing to everyone. For this, it is required to have a clear definition, along with the process defining the collection of data and their sources, and the calculations to be used in arriving at the measure.

Macy and Mirvis even developed operational definitions and computations for a number of behavioral outcomes.[19]

---

19. B. Macy and P. Mirvis, "Organizational Change Efforts: Methodologies for Assessing Organizational Effectiveness and Program Costs Versus Benefits," Evaluation Review 6, pp. 306–10. © 1982 by Sage Publications, Inc. Reprinted by permission of Sage Publications, Inc

This standardization makes it possible for measures to be compared at different points in time for an organization. It also makes it possible for the same measure to be compared across organizations. Research has been undertaken by experts towards the development of measures that are standardized and can be implemented across time periods, organizations, and industries.

It should be reliable

The value of the variable should closely represent the 'true' value of the variable that the OD intervention is trying to address.

Some variables are transparent and accurate. For example, if the intervention targets the number of bicycles produced in a factory, identifying and calculating the number of bicycles produced is a transparent variable that has no ambiguity.

In some cases, however, it may not be as straightforward. For example, if the target is the satisfaction level of employees with their jobs, asking them to rate their satisfaction may not produce reliable results as each person will provide a rating based on his/her perception and frame of mind. Whether a 7 on a scale of 10 is reflective of their level of satisfaction, or dissatisfaction will be unclear.

There are techniques available to OD practitioners to increase the reliability of such data.

When data collection is through a method that contains inherent biases, practitioners expand the collection process to include multiple methods. While it could create confusion if they all point in different directions, usually they can be used to triangulate on the issues. The various methods pointing in the same direction enhance confidence in the results.[20]

As an extension, the same data point could be collected in different ways. This is especially true while doing perception-based surveys when a question can be presented in different ways to the respondent. The science of psychometric evaluation is pressed into service for the development as well as analysis of such questionnaires. The discipline of psychometric evaluation has made rapid strides and is increasingly being used in designing questionnaires and surveys in organizations and for analyzing responses. Psychometric evaluations are also used for many other applications such as fitting people into suitable roles in an organization and evaluating the fit of a candidate with the company's culture and values.

Example

The measure of independence could be assessed through a set of questions placed at different points in the questionnaire:

1. I feel valued at work and encouraged to take decisions

2. My manager supports me when I take decisions

3. The job does not provide any opportunity for displaying initiative at the workplace

Responses to these three questions would provide an indication of either a consistent viewpoint or a mixed-up, confused perspective. Conclusions may be drawn based on psychometric tools used.

---

20. J. Corbin and A. Strauss, Basics of Qualitative Research, 4th ed. (Thousand Oaks, CA: Sage Publications, 2013); D. Miller, Handbook of Research Design and Social Measurement (Thousand Oaks, CA: Sage Publications, 1991); N. Denzin and Y. Lincoln, eds., Handbook of Qualitative Research (Thousand Oaks, CA: Sage Publications, 1994).

It should be a valid measure

Validity refers to the extent of a selected and measured variable reflecting and representing the variable it is being used to measure.

Surrogate variable

Where the target variable does not lend itself to direct measurement or isolation, other variables that could be reflective of the target variable are used. These are also known as surrogate variables.

For example, if employee morale is the target variable, there is no natural measure for it. Surveys and questionnaires can be used but they could have a user response bias. Sometimes, other variables could be used instead, like absenteeism, that do not have this bias and can be collected unobtrusively.

This, then, becomes a surrogate variable to measure employee morale.

If we are trying to address the issue of employee morale, and choose absenteeism as the variable that we would like to address, while the data collected will be reliable, as absenteeism is a discrete data point that can be easily collected and calculated, whether absenteeism is the right variable to use to measure employee morale would be the question. Thus, while the measure may be reliable, it may not be valid.

OD practitioners, again, rely on some techniques to enhance the validity of the measure.

Like in the case of reliability, here too the OD practitioner can adopt multiple measures for preliminary assessment. A positive correlation between these variables will increase confidence that the chosen variable is reflective of the variable that needs to be addressed.

Quiz

1. **The impact of an OD intervention can be measured:**

    a. Prior to launching it

    b. While it is being implemented

    c. Once implementation has been completed

2. **Implementation evaluation of an OD intervention is done:**

    a. Prior to launching it

    b. While it is being implemented

    c. Once implementation has been completed

3. **The parameters for evaluation of the impact of an OD intervention should be:**

    a. Decided at the time the OD intervention is being launched

    b. Decided during the implementation stage

    c. Decided once implementation has been completed

4. **The three corners of the Iron Triangle are:**

    a. Delivery, Quality, Time

    b. Time, Delivery, Cost

    c. Quality, Time, Cost

    d. Cost, Quality, Delivery

5. **Evaluation includes the measurement of:**

   a. Only target variable

   b. The target as well as connected variables

   c. Only the connected variables

6. **The measure of reliability is low when:**

   a. The value of the variable closely represents the 'true' value of the variable that the OD intervention is trying to address

   b. The value of the variable does not closely represent the 'true' value of the variable that the OD intervention is trying to address

   c. The measured variable reflects and represents the variable it is being used to measure

   d. The measured variable does not reflect and represent the variable it is being used to measure

7. **The measure of validity is high when:**

   a. The value of the variable closely represents the 'true' value of the variable that the OD intervention is trying to address

   b. The value of the variable does not closely represent the 'true' value of the variable that the OD intervention is trying to address

   c. The measured variable reflects and represents the variable it is being used to measure

   d. The measured variable does not reflect and represent the variable it is being used to measure

8. Where the target variable does not lend itself to direct measurement or isolation, other variables that could be reflective of the target variable are used. These are also known as surrogate variables.

   a. True

   b. False

9. If we are trying to address the issue of employee morale, and choose absenteeism as the variable that we would like to address, since there is no direct measure for morale, absenteeism becomes a:

   a. Surrogate variable

   b. Implementation variable

   c. Impact variable

   d. Delivery variable

10. Standardization definitions and calculations:

   a. make it possible for measures to be compared at different points in time for an organization

   b. make it possible for the same measure to be compared across organizations

   c. make it possible for the same measure to be compared across industries

   d. all of the above

Answers	1 – c	2 – b	3 – a	4 – d	5 – b
	6 – b	7 – c	8 – a	9 – a	10 – d

Chapter Summary

◆ Evaluation is the process through which an organization determines the level of success or failure of an OD intervention

◆ This process of evaluation is usually undertaken at two stages:

  • Implementation evaluation

  • Impact evaluation

◆ An evaluation measurement system is needed to assess the impact

◆ Measuring the target variable is important. Measuring other connected variables to ensure they do not slide while the target is improving is equally important.

◆ Measurement systems should be the product of the framework that is defined at the time an OD intervention is launched.

◆ Good measures should

  • Provide a stringent definition of operational variables

  • Be reliable – The value of the variable should closely represent the 'true' value of the variable that the OD intervention is trying to address

  • Be valid – The selected variable should be able to reflect and represent the variable it is being used to measure

This page is intentionally left blank

Chapter 8

Institutionalization

Once it has been established that the implementation has been successful and it is delivering the desired results, an effort needs to be made to institutionalize the process. The chapter will talk about what institutionalization means, and the need for it.

Key learning objectives include the reader's understanding of the following:

- The meaning of institutionalization

- The need for institutionalization

- How institutionalization benefits the organization

- Processes through which institutionalization is achieved

- Organizational parameters that could impede or facilitate the process.

- Challenges to the process.

- Measuring the level of institutionalization achieved.

8.1 Institutionalization and the Need for It

At some stage, the OD intervention, if deemed successful, will need to move into the DNA or bloodstream of the organization so that it can be practiced on an ongoing basis and stop being a project or an initiative.

While 'institutionalization' can conjure up images of submission to the administrative machinery, in the context of OD interventions, it is an important final step. One of the charges levied against many 'interventions' and 'projects' is that while all works well when the project phase is going on, with specific teams and members responsible for identified aspects and a clearly defined goal as the target, once the goal has been achieved and the project team disbanded, the organization reverts to its natural position, which is the position it was in before the OD intervention was initiated. Hence, the investment and effort put behind the effort comes to naught.

Hence, if lasting benefit is to be achieved, the new processes have to be institutionalized so that they become a part of the daily life of the organization and its employees.. It should become a part of job descriptions. It should be included in Standard Operating Procedures (SOPs). It should be included in employee Key Result Areas (KRAs).

Why should institutionalization be done? Why can the project or OD intervention phase not be a continuous phase?

The answer is fairly simple. An OD intervention is an added overhead for the organization. It pulls together a team of identified people, including some experts, to implement a planned change. If the people are external resources, they will cost money.

If the people are drawn from internal resources there will be a cost in terms of activities and tasks that they will not be able to do as a result of their involvement with this intervention. Both are costs and overheads for the organization. The organization agrees to take on this additional short-term cost because it is able to visualize a long-term benefit out of that investment. In other words, a Return on Investment (ROI) that is justified. If the project phase were to continue forever, it means that the additional cost and investment will continue forever and that there will never be a time when the organization will get an opportunity to get a return from it.

Why is there a need for successful implementation prior to institutionalization?

An unsuccessful implementation means that the intervention has not yielded the desired results. It might need to undergo some more cycles of review and implementation before its goals are attained. Conversely, it could also be declared unsuccessful and further efforts dropped. In either of these two cases, institutionalization serves no purpose. One will not institutionalize processes that are either unsuccessful or still being tried out to ensure the right combination emerges. The only exception might be a situation where the leadership team has approved a compromised goal as the updated goal which has been achieved. This could be on account of some environmental conditions changing during the intervention's timeline and impacting the goals initially defined.

8.2 Challenges with Institutionalization

Institutionalization appears to be the least studied part of the sequence of OD interventions. Most of the attention has been directed towards the earlier phases that deliver the results targeted. This has created a deficit in terms of models and examples to be followed in this phase.

The other challenge comes from OD practitioners themselves, and their focus on 'continuous change.' With continuous change as the defined desirable goal, the embedding of a new process into the workstream of an organization has, perhaps naturally, taken a backseat. Why implement a new process when it might change again in the near future, seems to be the philosophy.

It may be recollected that one of the efforts of OD interventions is to make the organization capable of handling future change. This then becomes another valid objective of both OD interventions as well as the process of institutionalization. In a way, this is an additional goal that is implicit in any OD intervention.

It is agreed that change will be ongoing. Hence, as part of the institutionalization process where we embed the new processes, strategies, and tasks into the workstream, can we also ensure that we are embedding a DNA that makes it ready to identify the need for planned change and go about implementing it in a structured manner?

With this, the need for institutionalization seems to again occupy its rightful position as the end point of a successful OD intervention.

8.3 Institutionalization-friendly Characteristics

Different OD interventions lend themselves differently to institutionalization, some promoting the process and some working against it.

The goal should be specific

The more specific the goal of an intervention, the greater the clarity with which it can be measured and evaluated. Specificity also lends itself much more easily to being communicated across the organization in a manner that it is understood in the same manner by everyone, leaving no room for ambiguity. It makes it easier for underlying tasks aimed at reaching that goal to be specified and followed by employees.

Tasks that line up to produce 1,000 light bulbs every hour are likely to be adopted by the employees much more easily than tasks that will lead to producing more light bulbs. Most sales teams prefer to define a goal for salespersons, however realistic or unrealistic it might be, rather than just leaving it as "do as much as you can."

Institutionalization is aided by standardization and conversion to a process

An intervention that can be specified in the form of discrete steps and processes will lend itself much more easily to adoption and repetition than a set of processes that cannot be clearly defined. While making it easier to be communicated across the organization, this feature will also facilitate individuals being tasked specifically with rewards being calculated in a transparent manner based on achievement of clearly defined steps and tasks.

How wide across the organization does the change go?

While this is a factor in institutionalization, there is no experience-based rule to say one is better than the other.

Interventions that target a specific, identified unit within the organization have the advantage of a well-defined scope and perhaps a more aligned unit of people who need to be introduced to the intervention, making it easier to implement. Similar attempts to do it organization-wide could meet pockets of resistance which could then spread across other units as well, thereby impairing the process.

On the other hand, there are also examples where institution-wide changes have worked well. The institutionalization process gained in strength with the initially targeted teams becoming champions of the process, aiding its spread across the organization.[21]

It should have internal support

An imposition is never long-lasting. If an OD intervention is the result of the decision of a few individuals in the organization, the resulting change might appear to be an imposition, and likely to face resistance from different units.

---

21. J. Martin and C. Siehl, "Organizational Cultures and Counterculture: An Uneasy Symbiosis," Organizational Dynamics (1983): 52–64; D. Meyerson and J. Martin, "Cultural Change: An Integration of Three Different Views," Journal of Management Studies 24 (1987): 623–47.

However, if the intervention is the result of either an organization-wide or department-wide consensus, the output and subsequent process of institutionalization will find advocates and supporters that will aid the flow of information as well as smoothen out the chinks and cracks that may have been overlooked.

While some experts feel that the OD expert being an internal person also aids the process, the jury is out on this subject. Many times, external consultants are able to achieve striking results when they drive consensus in the teams.

Leadership sponsorship

Power in an organization generally flows from the top. While some organizations may have a distributed responsibility for OD interventions, with multiple OD specialists and employees trained on interventions, it is helpful to have a sponsor who can smoothen the twists and turns in the road. There will be times of conflict between competing requirements for resources since the organization continues to work towards its long-term goals. It does not suspend them while the OD intervention is being planned and implemented. A senior person will be able to weigh in and do the allocation judiciously without being swayed by the pressure of delivering a healthy bottomline today. OD interventions could take time to deliver their ROI and hence need to be nurtured and sustained till then. Leadership support in this is always useful.

8.4 Institutionalization Processes

How does one go about the process of institutionalizing a change? What are the factors that affect the degree to which OD interventions are institutionalized?

Socialization of the message

The process of socialization refers to gaining widespread acceptance within the target organization. Done correctly, it translates to a process of change that is inclusive, and seems to be asked for by the teams themselves. They feel they are a part of the change process and not merely the ones implementing it based on orders from above.

Implementation of interventions is not a switch that can be turned on and off. It is an iterative process which entails much learning and experimentation even for the OD team. It is important that the impacted teams be kept well informed of developments. Otherwise, failure of some of the attempts can turn opinion against the implementation. Hence, socialization needs to be an ongoing process.

Commitment and ownership

The greater the commitment for the change from the recipient team/unit, the greater the likelihood of success. While there are many initiatives that could lead to building of commitment, it remains an essential ingredient for successful institutionalization. It should also be kept in mind that while building commitment is a gradual process, it can come apart very easily, much like trust between individuals.

As we have discussed in other places in this book, the greater the ownership of the people impacted by change, the greater the chance of success of the change. Ownership is, in a way, equivalent to commitment.

Reward and recognition

While all organizations want employees who will work for their love of the job, employees also need to pay bills and often support their families and dependents. They work for satisfaction. They work to be a part of something larger than themselves. They work for social acceptance. They work for recognition. But above all, they work for money.

The alignment of the reward and recognition programs in the organization towards the behavior and parameters required by the changed processes is an important step in this direction. The good practices that HR managers usually follow while instituting a reward and recognition system remain constant and need to be borne in mind while designing reward structures that are based on the behavior and performance demanded by the changed system and process.

Spread the message of change

Through a process referred to as diffusion, change can be transferred between systems; in the organizational context, from one part of the organization to another, and then another, and so on.

What it does is build a larger base of support for the change being implemented, rather than the change running counter to the desired behavior and performance parameters in other parts, and hence feeling the pressure to continue to conform by reverting to their old ways.

Change is more likely to succeed when it makes sense. In other words, it is beneficial to the organization as well as its members. Acceptance of the change through the process of diffusion also serves to demonstrate the acceptability of the change being implemented, not in one unit, but across the organization.

Make it iterative

Institutionalization requires working with people more than anything else. People are unpredictable and different people have different perspectives and responses. The process becomes one of trial and error to some extent. The organization keeps learning while progressing.

Other factors can also create resistance such as environmental changes, leadership changes, change in technologies, comfort with status quo, etc.

The process of institutionalization needs to be sensitive to these pressures and demonstrate the flexibility that may be needed to overcome such distractions. It might even call for renewed rounds of socialization and commitment reinforcement. In short, the organization has to be prepared to make the process of institutionalization an iterative one.

8.5 Measuring the Level of Institutionalization

An organization must measure. It needs to consistently evaluate the effectiveness of its initiatives and whether its resources are being allocated judiciously. While the evaluation of an OD intervention is done at the eponymous stage, it is also an ongoing exercise. It also helps the organization in measuring the longevity of the change, whether it has been really embedded into the DNA or the organization has started displaying signs of reverting back to the status quo.

Employee knowledge and behavior

Do employees continue to have knowledge of the new, expected behaviors and continue to perform them? What proportion of the people are doing so? Is it displaying a reducing or increasing trend? Does this apply only to the frequently performed actions or are the infrequent actions expected also remembered and performed?

Private versus public position

Many employees, in a formal group setting, are unlikely to voice their disagreement with the official position unless it hurts them deeply and personally. Most of the time they will go along with the flow. If their private position is at odds with their public position, they are likely to lapse into old behaviors as they do not really buy into the changed processes. Private acceptance, on the other hand, results in positive behavioral outcomes. While it may not be easy, attempts should be made to draw out private positions.

Social consensus

In addition to private positions, social positions and views also become important in institutionalization. Social groups are a part of being human and form in every setting where there are people. These social groups act as binding factors for people. A shared sense of comfort, belonging, and agreement is likely to spur adoption.

Quiz

1. **An OD intervention can be considered completed when**

   a. The process of Evaluation has been completed

   b. The OD expert has started the next intervention

   c. The process of Institutionalization has been completed

2. **The main purpose of institutionalization could be:**

   a. Releasing the OD expert to work on other interventions

   b. Embedding the new processes and systems into the workstream of the organization

   c. Going back to the status quo

3. **Changes in which of the following may indicate that the institutionalization process has been completed?**

   a. Job Descriptions

   b. Standard Operating Procedures (SOPs)

   c. Key Result Areas (KRAs) of individual employees

   d. All of the above

4. **If the goal of an intervention is specific, will it impede or help the process of institutionalization?**

   a. Impede

   b. Help

   c. Don't know

5. **Socialization is a one-off process and best done at one time.**

   a. Agree

   b. Disagree

6. **Institutionalization is likely to be best achieved when the target of change is:**

   a. A single functional unit

   b. Multiple divisions

   c. The entire organization

   d. Cannot say

7. **Individual rewards and recognition cease to be important when institutionalization of an OD intervention is done.**

   a. Agree

   b. Disagree

8. **Which of the following characteristics are expected to aid the process of institutionalization? (Choose all applicable)**

   a. Having an external sponsor

   b. Programmability

   c. Internal Support for the intervention

   d. Having a senior sponsor

9. Promoting the new, good practices in the larger organization, even the units which are not a target for change, help develop a wellspring of support for the new processes and behaviors. This process is known as:

   a. Socialization

   b. Commitment

   c. Diffusion

   d. Sensing and Calibration

10. Measurement is done at the stage of Evaluation. Once institutionalized, there is no further need for any measurement.

    a. True

    b. False

Answers	1 – c	2 – b	3 – d	4 – b	5 – b
	6 – d	7 – b	8 – b, c, d	9 – c	10 – b

Chapter Summary

◆ Institutionalization is an important last step that helps in embedding the new processes into the workstream of the organization, making them regular processes and delivering ROI benefit.

◆ Challenges include lack of attention to this phase of the OD intervention and the belief in continuous change taking away the importance of implementing new processes.

◆ Characteristics that determine how friendly the intervention is to institutionalization of new processes are:

- How specific are the goals

- Capacity for standardization and conversion to a process

- How wide across the organization does the change go?

- Internal support

- Leadership sponsorship

◆ The factors that affect the degree to which OD interventions are institutionalized are:

- Socialization of the message

- Commitment and ownership

- Reward and recognition

- Spread the message of change

- Make it iterative

Chapter **9**

The Making of an OD Practitioner

E ven though organizations have an independent legal existence, they act only through their human agents. These human agents have different roles to play, one of them being that of an OD practitioner. This chapter fleshes out the role of an OD practitioner.

Key learning objectives include the reader's understanding of the following:

- Definition of key terms: cultural awareness, six degrees of separation, three degrees of separation, social movements

- Different types of OD practitioners

- Competencies of OD practitioners

- Core skills and knowledge of OD practitioners

- Expectations of an OD practitioner

- Characteristics of individuals who perform the OD role

- Challenges that practitioners have to face from time to time

9.1 The OD Practitioner

Will I make a good OD practitioner?

This question no doubt occurs to people who have developed an interest in the subject and are interested in taking up a career in it. And rightfully so, since OD may be called an emerging profession, and not yet an established one like that of doctors, lawyers, engineers, and accountants.

The role of an OD practitioner has also developed along two parallel lines, as external consultants, and as internal team members. It seems to depend on the preference of the organization as well as that of the individual, in terms of which model is preferred. While the theory and knowledge may not change, the role is likely to be different at different stages of the OD intervention. Both will eventually require participation from team members as well as the sponsorship of the senior leadership if their work is to achieve any form of success.

The term itself has wide application. It is used to refer to several different types of OD practitioners even though it is believed that the distinctions are blurring.

OD professional

This is the most obvious group of people referred to as OD practitioners. For them, OD is a profession. They could be employed by an organization and work exclusively for them in multiple interventions as per need, or operate as an external consultant who could be hired by an organization with a need for one.

It must be remembered that OD professionals are also human beings and hence, even for the sake of professional benefit, need to be adept at humanistic values such as honesty and integrity. As organizational complexity has increased, so has the domain coverage of OD professionals freely drawing upon other disciplines like Psychology, Sociology, Statistics and Quality Systems for solutions.

Specialists in related disciplines

OD is known to draw extensively from other disciplines such as quality, organizational design, employee reward systems, etc. As these disciplines have developed, so has the number of people specializing in them. These specialists are developing their expertise in the field of OD through the work they do in OD interventions with other OD professionals. As a result, much of the application of their own skills and specialization takes the form and shape of an OD intervention, since an OD intervention is seen as a good model to bring about any type of planned change in an organization. These specialists in related disciplines then also qualify to be termed as OD professionals.

Managers

The science of OD is implemented in an organizational context. There are people in the organization where the intervention is developed and implemented who will be involved in many aspects of the intervention. The process usually requires widespread participation along with training, so that the change is not an imposition, but an internally created movement that has a greater chance of success through greater ownership.

Through participation in OD interventions, many of the employees and managers in the organization develop their skills in the discipline and become comfortable enough to initiate OD interventions on their own in their responsibility areas. Recent studies point to this group of people being catalysts for the rapid change taking place in organizations. Moreover, being the impacted parties, the change they seek to bring about does not suffer from a lack of buy-in as occasionally happens in case of forced change. Some of these managers either become full-time OD practitioners or switch between the two.

9.2 Competencies

How does one nail down the competencies required in an OD professional? Is there even a standard list possible or do OD practitioners come in various shapes and forms?

An attempt was made in which practitioners were asked to update a dynamic (growing) list of competencies.

A set of well-known practitioners created a list of 187 statements in nine areas of practice, to reflect their view on relevant competencies. Data was then collected from 364 OD practitioners for the listed competencies. An analysis and classification of the results suggested a final set of 23 competencies, a collective of required personal characteristics as well as knowledge and skills required to effect planned change.

Some of the top competencies that emerged were:

- ability to evaluate change

- working with large-scale change efforts

- creating implementation plans

- managing diversity

- self-mastery; this emerged as the most important competence and reaffirmed the belief of OD experts of self-knowledge and awareness forming the basis of successful practice.

Another attempt was sponsored by the Organization Development and Change Division of the Academy of Management.[22]

Over 40 OD practitioners and researchers worked to develop the list that was divided between:

- foundation competencies that included knowledge from organizational behavior, psychology, group dynamics, management and organization theory, research methods, and business practices.

---

22. C. Worley and G. Varney, "A Search for a Common Body of Knowledge for Master's Level Organization Development and Change Programs — An Invitation to Join the Discussion," Academy of Management ODC Newsletter (Winter 1998): 1–4

- core competencies that included knowledge of organization design, organization research, system dynamics, OD history, and theories and models for change; they also involve the skills needed to manage the consulting process: to analyze and diagnose systems, to design and choose interventions, to facilitate processes, to develop clients' capability to manage their own change, and to evaluate organization change.

9.3 Core Skills and Knowledge

On the basis of the aforementioned studies, along with several others, the following have been determined to be the core competencies OD practitioners are expected to possess in order to be effective:

Intrapersonal skills

In a people-driven discipline, the ability to manage oneself acquires relevance. At each step, decisions need to be made: regarding the data to be collected, people to be spoken with, methods of analysis, and many others. An OD practitioner who does not have the confidence in himself/herself to be taking these decisions, and the ability to draw upon one's reservoirs of knowledge and skills in times of need will find it to be an uphill task. While tools, technology, and models can be referred to, what works best in a given situation will need to be decided. An OD practitioner often has to plow a lonely furrow and it can be a stressful job.

Interpersonal skills

Equally important is the ability to work with people. Large organizations require large volumes of work and effort, whether it is for data collection or socialization. The OD practitioner can do only so much on his/her own. It is imperative that the team involved in the exercise be empowered to carry out tasks and make decisions. This, in any case, is a recommended best practice as it leads to greater ownership on part of impacted teams. Otherwise, it becomes an imposition and often faces pushback from the organizational teams. The OD practitioner needs to lead without being an appointed leader.

Counseling and consultation skills

This could be seen as an extension of the previous skill. In order for interventions to be designed that are suitable, the OD expert needs to develop an understanding of the situation without, in most cases, having worked in that unit. Thus, there will always be team members he works with who are more knowledgeable about the process and function. He does not know as much as them, but needs the consultant's ability to ask the right questions, and draw out the right responses, based on which he will be able to develop a plan that is palatable to the 'insiders.' It does not matter whether the OD expert is an employee or an external consultant. Even when he is an employee, he will frequently need to work in teams about which he has limited knowledge. Moreover, he needs to be able to work with different levels in the organization.

Knowledge of the subject

Lastly, it is expected that the OD practitioner brings knowledge about the subject to the table. It is expected that he is familiar with the theories and the processes experts before him have gone through in developing and fine-tuning them. What we don't want is a practitioner who learns from his errors at each step. He should be learning also from errors others in his profession have made before him.

9.4 Expectations of an OD Practitioner

It is important to understand the expectations and demands that will be placed on you as an OD professional.

Adopt a position of marginality

Marginality refers to straddling the fine line between multiple groups of people, multiple divisions in an organization, and even between the organization and one of its divisions. An OD practitioner is expected to do so without being by one versus the other. A marginal position sometimes referred to as 'fence-sitters' in uncharitable terms, has come to acquire importance with the understanding of an OD practitioner's role. Studies also find that some people are better at playing a marginal role than others.

It will make emotional demands

Change is always difficult. An OD practitioner's role is mostly about change. Being seen as a representation of the change that is dreaded by many is an emotionally responsible and demanding role. Hence, the skill-set of an OD practitioner will not merely be limited to problem-solving and functional knowledge. It will include soft skills like emotional intelligence and the ability to leverage them for better decision-making. It often helps make better decisions by recognizing information that is often discarded by models and theories.[23]

Needs to leverage one's own as well as organizational knowledge

In some ways, this is a classic people-management role. The OD practitioner not only needs to bring the best out of people but also needs to be able to dig deep into their reservoirs of native knowledge and intelligence and stitch together the most appropriate solution.

Typically, the consultant needs to begin by drawing out organizational knowledge and layering it with the knowledge and skills of OD to determine the most suitable interventions.

9.5 Ethical Issues that Confront Practitioners

Being a human-driven activity, like with all human-driven activities, there are occasions when the practitioner can be confronted by dilemmas of an ethical nature. While eventually it is left to the discretion of each individual how they are to be

---

23. C. Lundberg and C. Young, "A Note on Emotions and Consultancy," Journal of Organizational Change Management 14 (2001): 530–38; A. Carr, "Understanding Emotion and Emotionality in a Process of Change," Journal of Organizational Change Management 14 (2001): 421–36.

handled, based on his/her own moral compass, knowing about them places one in a better position to recognize them when the occasion does come. This may hopefully position the consultant better so that he does not succumb to temptation.

Misguiding the organization

This could be of various types, usually meant to increase the opportunity of the practitioner deriving financial gains from doing so. He could suggest interventions in situations where no intervention is needed. He could suggest interventions that might be difficult to evaluate. He could suggest repeated cycles of interventions where one might be sufficient.

Theft of Data

For an organization, data is valuable. An OD practitioner gets access to data of the organization when he signs up as their consultant. He is also well placed to ask for more and more data in the name of the intervention. Generally, there would be agreements in place that will specify how data can be accessed and used. They could misuse the data directly, which is an obvious criminal activity. The consultant should also take ownership of how data is made available to other members of the team and ensure there are adequate controls around it.

Coercion

Coercion can occur in different ways. An OD expert, during the process of an intervention, is seemingly in a position of some power as the organization looks up to him for a type of deliverance. OD practitioners must be in possession of a steady moral compass which they refer to in times of stress that could lead to compromising on the values of the discipline.

Coercion need not be visible or violent. In the event of a clash of opinions, is the practitioner being enticed by the prospect of creating a case, based on his superior knowledge, so that the intervention moves in the direction of his choice? Is he enticed by the prospect of withholding services because the client does not have the same vision or goal?

Technical weakness

There could be a tendency to press on with an intervention despite the OD practitioner not possessing the adequate skills and experience required by the intervention. Calling for help from another, more qualified practitioner might seem like a weakness that he would rather avoid. Sometimes the expert could also let his own comfort level with different types of analysis and interventions guide the process, regardless of what will be beneficial for the organization and what would work best in the given situation.

Quiz

1. Which of the following can be considered to be the newest profession?

    a. Accountant

    b. OD practitioner

    c. Doctor

    d. Engineer

2. One of the reasons OD appears to be an attractive profession is that there is the promise of great variety in interventions.

    a. True

    b. False

3. The term OD practitioner should not be used to refer to which of the following sets of people?

    a. OD professional

    b. Leadership team of the organization

    c. Specialist in a related discipline who works on OD interventions

    d. Managers and employees who work with OD specialists and develop their skills

4. **Interventions run by which of the following sets of people are likely to witness a higher level of acceptance from the impacted units compared to the others?**

   a. OD professional

   b. Leadership team of the organization

   c. Specialist in a related discipline who works on OD interventions

   d. Managers and employees who work with OD specialists and develop their skills

5. **How many competencies were identified by Worley and his colleagues in their study of 364 practitioners?**

   a. 16

   b. 18

   c. 23

   d. 74

6. **The most important competency that emerged from the study by Worley and colleagues was:**

   a. ability to evaluate change

   b. working with large-scale change efforts

   c. creating implementation plans

   d. managing diversity

   e. self-mastery

7. The study sponsored by the Organization Development and Change Division of the Academy of Management for identification of competencies divided them into the following categories:

    a. Foundation and Core

    b. Core and Expert

    c. Basic, Medium and Expert

    d. Expert and Champion

8. **Select the 'core' competencies from the list. (Multiple choices can be made)**

    a. organization design

    b. organization research

    c. psychology

    d. management theory

9. **An attempt by the OD practitioner to misguide the organization is most likely to be caused by the desire to:**

    a. Lead the organization to ruin

    b. Hide one's incompetence

    c. Derive financial gain

    d. Set up a competing organization

10. The OD practitioner, through his conduct and management, is expected to control the theft of data:

a. by other participants

b. by himself

c. by other participants as well as himself

d. by nobody – he has no responsibility for it

Answers	1 – b	2 – a	3 – b	4 – d	5 – c
	6 – e	7 – a	8 – a, b	9 – c	10 – c

Chapter Summary

◆ In common parlance, the term OD practitioner is applied to three sets of professionals. These three types are:

- People whose core specialization is in the field of OD

- People who have a specialization in a related field like quality or employee reward systems that work closely with OD as a result of which they develop the skills to lead OD interventions

- People, usually managers in organizations, who develop expertise in the field of OD as a result of their participation in OD interventions

◆ Attempts have been made to identify skills relevant for the profession. One such attempt classifies skills into Foundation and Core skills. Another study identified self-mastery as the most important skill for an OD practitioner.

◆ Skills applicable for all practitioners:

1. intrapersonal skills

2. interpersonal skills

3. general consultation skills

4. knowledge of OD theory.

◆ Expectations of an OD professional:

- Adopt a position of marginality

- It will make emotional demands

- Needs to leverage one's own as well as organizational knowledge

◆ OD specialists may face value dilemmas in trying to jointly optimize human benefits and organization performance. They must guard against:

- Misrepresentation

- Misuse of Data

- Coercion

- Technical weakness

Notes

www.ingramcontent.com/pod-product-compliance
Lightning Source LLC
Chambersburg PA
CBHW060301220326
41598CB00027B/4192